MW00624027

"To say *From Isolation to* right, but its eloquence an ~~~~~~~ ~~~~~~~. To say something is reflective and eloquent about someone so profound as Bonhoeffer was in *Life Together* is to give us fresh eyes to read Bonhoeffer's classic all over again, as if for the first time. Reading Werntz's reflections on Bonhoeffer amid isolation makes me ache for life together with my brothers and sisters in Christ."

—**Scot McKnight**, Northern Seminary

"For some time we North Americans have celebrated our freedom. It turns out that what we have gotten is loneliness, meaninglessness, and, in Werntz's language, isolation. When we come to church, we just bring our isolation with us. What's the cure? Community, carved out by Christ among his disciples, here refracted through Dietrich Bonhoeffer's luminous witness. Werntz sees clearly what ails us and the cure God has already given."

—**Jason Byassee**, Vancouver School of Theology

"Through much of the modern period, Christianity adapted itself to succor the needs of atomized individuals at the mercy of profound social change. Unwittingly, this accommodation took the state of isolation as given, and thus isolation ironically repeated itself in the solutions on offer. Whether in conservative-reactionary or liberal-progressive forms, modernized Christianity modeled identity either as the self's assertion of sovereignty or the self's absorption into a collectivity. But according to Werntz's welcome construction of a theological alternative inspired by the work of Dietrich Bonhoeffer, the Christian gospel is essentially about the formation of community in Christ, which interprets the state of isolation as the consequence of sinful alienation from God the Creator. Resolving this spiritual alienation, community in Christ cascades out into the world in a series of joyful exchanges on the trajectory of beloved community."

—**Paul R. Hinlicky**, Roanoke College; Evanjelická Bohoslovecká Fakulta, Univerzita Komenského, Bratislava, Slovakia

"In a moment where we are relearning what community is and could be, Werntz offers us language for what was building our walls of isolation, even prior to pandemic quarantines and a socially distant reality. *From Isolation to Community* is a vital book for helping us to rediscover the promise and hope of life together."

—**Brian Bantum**, Garrett-Evangelical Theological Seminary

"There is no shortage of books on the thought of Dietrich Bonhoeffer. Nor is there any shortage of books on church and ministry in our contemporary moment. But books that can put these together are few and far between. Yet here is one! *From Isolation to Community* does so marvelously. With dexterity and depth Werntz brings Bonhoeffer to life in a way that will help churches faithfully minister in this time. It's a valuable read."

—**Andrew Root**, Luther Seminary; author
of *Churches and the Crisis of Decline*

FROM ISOLATION
TO COMMUNITY

FROM ISOLATION TO COMMUNITY

A RENEWED VISION
FOR CHRISTIAN LIFE TOGETHER

MYLES WERNTZ

Baker Academic
a division of Baker Publishing Group
Grand Rapids, Michigan

Published by Baker Academic
a division of Baker Publishing Group
PO Box 6287, Grand Rapids, MI 49516-6287
www.bakeracademic.com

Printed in the United States of America

Library of Congress Cataloging-in-Publication Data
Names: Werntz, Myles, author.
Title: From isolation to community : a renewed vision for Christian life together / Myles Werntz.
Description: Grand Rapids, Michigan : Baker Academic, a division of Baker Publishing Group, [2022] | Includes index.
Identifiers: LCCN 2021040499 | ISBN 9781540965059 (paperback) | ISBN 9781540965370 (casebound) | ISBN 9781493435135 (ebook) | ISBN 9781493435142 (pdf)
Subjects: LCSH: Communities—Religious aspects—Christianity. | Church. | Bonhoeffer, Dietrich, 1906–1945. Gemeinsames Leben. | Christian life. | Christian communities.
Classification: LCC BV4517.5 .W47 2022 | DDC 255—dc23
LC record available at https://lccn.loc.gov/2021040499

Scripture quotations are from the New Revised Standard Version of the Bible, copyright © 1989 National Council of the Churches of Christ in the United States of America. Used by permission. All rights reserved.

Baker Publishing Group publications use paper produced from sustainable forestry practices and post-consumer waste whenever possible.

22   23   24   25   26   27   28   7   6   5   4   3   2   1

To Chip Conyers,
who told me to stay

[People] acquire the habit of always considering themselves as standing alone, and they are apt to imagine that their whole destiny is in their own hands. . . . [Democracy] throws him back forever upon himself alone, and threatens in the end to confine him entirely within the solitude of his own heart.

—Alexis de Tocqueville, 1835

We are all specialized forms of survivors. . . . We lack what we fundamentally need and forge ahead regardless, hurriedly hiding our wounds, disguising our ineptitude, bluffing our way through our weaknesses. No one—especially not a pastor—should lose sight of that truth.

—Michel Faber, *The Book of Strange New Things*

As you therefore have received Christ Jesus the Lord, continue to live your lives in him, rooted and built up in him and established in the faith.

—Colossians 2:6–7

CONTENTS

ACKNOWLEDGMENTS

This was a book written in reflection of and gratitude for having experienced some of what I express here, and partly in aspiration for what the church is called to be. My life's vocation thus far has been to teach the church's future leaders, to help shepherd seminarians into church life, and it is difficult to lead someone to see what you yourself have not. Such is the case here: the gift of Christian community is rare and good and true, and I have seen it in many forms: in college dorm rooms, on summer camp staffs, in attempts at Christian communal living and through local churches. Mistakes were made. And much joy was shared.

The number of people who, during my teaching of seminarians for the last ten years, have formed me and helped me to know and see the things described here is too many for me to name individually. The faculties of George W. Truett Theological Seminary, Palm Beach Atlantic University's School of Ministry, Logsdon Seminary, and Abilene Christian University's Graduate School of Theology have all in their own ways contributed to this book, as they have all been places of nurture, attention, and care for Christ's body, the church. It is a privilege to do what I do, to spend my days among people committed to the future of Christ's church while acknowledging that its future is ultimately in the hands of God.

Dietrich Bonhoeffer, the main interlocutor of this book, has been a theological companion for many years. On the way, Barry Harvey, Claire Hein, Wyatt Miles, Josh Carpenter, Chris W. Moore, Jordan Mallory, Jenny C. Howell, Michael Mawson, Christopher Dodson, and the participants of the Bonhoeffer and Society section of the American Academy of Religion have been instructive for me; the students at Logsdon Seminary who suffered through my course on Bonhoeffer as interpreter of Scripture were particularly faithful fellow readers, though all interpretive errors remain mine. Todd Cederberg, rector of St. Mary's Episcopal Church in Stuart, Florida, gave me the gift of leading St. Mary's in a Lenten series over *Life Together*, during which many of these thoughts began to form. Bob Hosack, James Korsmo, and Robert Banning at Baker Academic provided invaluable assistance in shepherding this project to completion. The saints of Calvary Baptist Church in Waco, Texas; Memorial Presbyterian Church in West Palm Beach, Florida; and First Baptist Church in Abilene, Texas, have borne witness to the difficulty and promise of Christian community. And Sarah Martin-Werntz, as always, has made our home a school of holiness, leading our family in hospitality and grace.

In 2004, as he was dying of cancer, I sat in the kitchen of Abda Johnson "Chip" Conyers, my first theology professor, to ask advice about starting a PhD program. I had done two degrees in Baptist universities and was hesitant to stay at Baylor University to do a PhD, for it would mark me forever as a Baptist, bound to be a part of this people. Other options were possible, and at that point, I was of the opinion that an academic needed diversity and breadth rather than confessional commitment. I confessed my worry about belonging to a church tradition that strongly, to which he responded simply, "Perhaps that's because this is where you need to be."

It was not the answer I sought, but it was the one I needed. I think of that moment frequently because in that conversation with Dr. Conyers I learned the wisdom of being committed to one place and to one people, with the hope that it will be stronger than before, and that communion with Christ is both a matter of God's gifts and of leaning into the difficult way of commitment over time. It is in Chip Conyers's blessed memory that I dedicate this book.

This book was begun in dark times, but when we commit ourselves to a people over time, not all times can be good ones. It was written in part to remind me of the grace of Christian community, in a time when many things spoke of isolation, to write myself into hope. May it be something of that for the reader as well.

INTRODUCTION

NAMING OUR PROBLEM:
ISOLATION AND THE HUMAN CONDITION

A great deal is at stake with how we as Christians name both our problems and our solutions. For if we name the problem too trivially, we wind up offering an unserious solution. It is for no small reason that Scripture opens up our situation in such stark terms: "death," "corruption," "evil." If we named what afflicts us in light ways, we would offer trivial solutions to challenges that run all the way down: to misname this is to misname our cure as well.

The story of the world, Augustine tells us, is one of both grace and division, of Abel versus Cain, the City of God versus the Earthly City: this common gift of creation and its division into light and dark is at the headwaters of the stories we tell about creation. As inheritors of a common curse and destined for a common cure, we the people of God live in overlapping ways with our neighbors as the church bears out its witness. The way that sin appears, then, is not one that is restricted to the world outside the church, insofar as all people share in Adam's lineage, all people repeating the story of the fall again and again. And so, to be the people of the church means to recognize that, in our healing, we will be tempted again and again to slip back into old patterns and tempted to repeat the ways in which sin fractures the world.

In this book, we look at how this pattern of division happens in and through church practices, following the guidance primarily of Dietrich Bonhoeffer, and we will name that pattern *isolation*. With the German martyr as our guide, we will begin a process of reframing our vision of church, moving away from isolation and toward *community*, a form of life together that mirrors the existence creation is called toward before God.

Loneliness and even *estrangement* we are familiar with, but *isolation*? Is this too strong a term to describe the ways in which sin afflicts our common life? The skepticism of this nomenclature, I think, is twofold. First, it may come from a fear that this prioritizes sin as a fundamental reality of creation rather than grace. It is, after all, only because God sustains the world that we are able to name isolation clearly, as a falling away from our intended state as creatures. We were created for communion with God, and isolation is what we settle for and, as we shall see, unwittingly calibrate our experience of church to. But in order to see the way home, we must name the problem for what it is.

The second reason to be skeptical of the term *isolation* to describe the human condition may come from associating isolation with an extreme situation: that of prisoners in solitary confinement, of nomads living without another human soul. But these are simply isolation—as a theological reality—taking a dramatic physical shape. *Isolation*, as used in this book, refers not merely to a phenomenon but to a state that dictates how we in turn view the self and the activities that we do. Isolation names a condition in which, because of sin, the human exists divided from others and from God. Because of this division, we share a common world sustained by God, but we view one another as competitors in that world, each of us closed off, threatened by all others, and sustained fundamentally by our own efforts.

While *loneliness* describes a feeling that ebbs and flows with the presence of others, *isolation*—a pervasive state—better describes our state under sin, even when we are in the presence of others. Loneliness is, in other words, the harbinger of isolation, sending a message to remind us that this feeling of distance from others that we endure temporally is an echo of a far more serious situation. In using the term *isolation* throughout this book, I am naming the way sin permeates the world and the ways this condition then leads us to structure the world to try to overcome or compensate for that condition.

It is *isolation* that better describes the complex way in which sin divides human beings from God and one another, distancing them from the goodness and benefit of the God who is our source and from others, through whom we receive these good gifts. It is *isolation* that describes the distance between humans and the earth, the unfamiliarity and antagonism that one creature exhibits toward another creature. It is *isolation* that names the experience of life as being bracketed by an almost inescapable aloneness, even if others encounter a semblance of who we are or if we experience relief from loneliness for years on end. Describing creation in this way does not mean that we do not share a common language, heritage, or interests, nor does it entail denying that creation is upheld and sustained by the God who is working for its reconciliation. It means that, theologically, humans live in ways that are always seeking to overcome a perpetual distance between us, to restore communion where there remains rupture, and that we frequently attempt a restoration which misunderstands the problem.

The Problem of Seeing Isolation

Popular discussions have tended toward viewing isolation as something that is "out there," perpetuated by cultures that trade in individualism and self-discovery, fraying the best of our social bonds and shared values.[1] But this is not the whole truth: isolation, as a feature

1. Sociological classics such as Robert Putnam's *Bowling Alone: The Collapse and Revival of American Community* (New York: Simon & Schuster, 2020) and psychological accounts such as Jonathan Haidt's *The Righteous Mind: Why Good People Are Divided by Politics and Religion* (New York: Vintage, 2012) and Sebastian Junger's *Tribe: On Homecoming and Belonging* (New York: Twelve Books, 2016) are indicative of this class of titles, analyzing the ways in which certain cultural elements contribute to social division. Mitigation strategies, such as in Noreena Hertz's *The Lonely Century: How to Restore Human Connection in a World That's Pulling Apart* (New York: Currency, 2021), follow the presumption of these titles: that what is needed is a kind of cultural renewal that utilizes the technological tools at hand to mend cultural isolation. It is here that titles such as Zerlina Maxwell's *The End of*

of creaturely life under sin, afflicts the church as well, and the ways in which we practice church. In chapter 2, we will go more into detail here: to attain a vision of what is at stake with seeing the church as a community, we must reckon with the problem of having dedicated ourselves broadly to the tasks of mending the world—overcoming the divisions and isolation within the world—while allowing isolation to permeate and shape our own vision of church life.

If isolation—the state in which we exist, dividing ourselves from one another and from God—permeates even the life of the church, then we can see isolation appearing in our church life in two different, polar-opposite forms. This will be more fully discussed in chapter 1 and will be an assumed feature of the later chapters in which we discuss church practice, but let us introduce the idea here. Following Bonhoeffer, we can see that there are two faces to isolation: that of the *crowd* and that of the *individual*.

In the crowd, the person obscures their isolation by joining their voice with a collective that covers them, providing them with a shelter against being alone. As we shall see, this frequently comes hand in hand with strong leaders who promise vision and shelter from this isolation, bringing additional problems. It may seem counterintuitive to name *isolation* as present in collectives. But as Augustine reminds us, this social form hides internal divisions, frequently set aside for tactical successes, such that the most powerful of empires are but imagined communities construed to stave off the tide of isolation that will not be set aside forever.[2] To see Augustine's point, one need

---

White Politics: How to Heal Our Liberal Divide (New York: Hachette Books, 2020) both accurately assess a phenomenon (the decline of Anglo-dominant politics and the ensuing cultural fragmentation that has emerged) while erroneously looking to the political anthropology of liberalism (which assumes the autonomy of the human person) as the solution to cultural division.

2. Augustine, in describing the "city of Cain," the stand-in for all human societies, writes:

> This city is often divided against itself by litigations, wars, quarrels, and such victories as are either life-destroying or short-lived. For each part of it that arms against another part of it seeks to triumph over the nations through itself in bondage to vice. If, when it has conquered, it is inflated with pride, its victory is life-destroying; but if it turns its thoughts upon the common casualties of our mortal condition, and is rather anxious concerning the disasters that may befall it than elated with the successes already achieved, this victory,

only look to the ways in which the dynasties of Scripture are undone by those closest to them, or to the ways in which the intimacies of the church are the occasion for egregious harms: if members are not mediated to one another in Christ's body, even the most valued social bonds will revert back to the law of Adam, of prioritizing the self over against all others. The best and most natural of bonds—of family, of marriage, of friendship—will disintegrate, apart from God's knitting them together.

If crowds are one face of isolation, the triumphant *individual* provides us a different face. For if the crowd hides our isolation and lack of connection in one way, individualism is its mirror image, championing what the crowd hides. Individuals—who must make all decisions for themselves—find themselves thrown into the world, with only the courageous able to navigate it, on the strength of will and fortitude. In this form, isolation appears as the demand to take on the burden of the world, carrying the weight of being self-made and self-sustained. While there is certainly value in speaking of personal agency and virtue, of the singular Daniel who defies an empire or of the Paul who preaches to the mob, this obscures the fact that Daniel is not Daniel by himself, nor is Paul the singular figure against all odds; rather, they are bearers of a community, shaped by and representing a covenantal people. The courageous individual, as construed in contemporary discourse, is more our accommodation to the fall, making the best of a bad situation, than a person functioning as humans were meant to.[3]

---

though of a higher kind, is still only short-lived; for it cannot abidingly rule over those whom it has victoriously subjugated. But the things which this city desires cannot justly be said to be evil, for it is itself, in its own kind, better than all other human good. (*City of God*, trans. Henry Bettenson [New York: Penguin Books, 1972], 599)

Put differently, the crowd is a façade, for no sooner does the city achieve some measure of social cohesion than it divides against itself.

3. This is not to catalog all those who are divided from others, such as the prisoner or the shut-in. Those divided from others, but unwillingly so, might prefer to name this problem "loneliness," to say that our singularity is not something to be celebrated but to be lamented and mourned. The lonely do not look to turn their singularity into a strength, nor do they envision themselves as able to carry the weight of the world on their shoulders: they ask only for company. But loneliness—the feeling that accompanies being unknown and unseen by others—unlike the more complex isolation, can be alleviated for a time by the presence of another: a visit, a long-needed phone call, a quick conversation in the hall that delves beneath the surface. The problem is

As churches, we frequently mistakenly address this condition of isolation as loneliness by setting the table for people to speak with one another, to learn from one another, to plan outings, cultivate friendships, and find connection in similar interests, and in doing so, frequently think we have abated the deeper problem. But these antidotes to loneliness fail in time. Rome's victories turn to ash as it turns on itself; the lonely are sustained by the memory of their friends for only a season as the companionship is eroded by time; relationships made in church deteriorate when one reason for aggregating ourselves within church replaces another. This issue of isolation is not one that can be resolved by hiding in crowds, by the temporary balm of company, or by somehow finding the resources to face the world alone. And so this is the claim that, theologically, we make: in a world after sin, we are creatures vexed by isolation, even if we live amid crowds of people, close to friends, with families for decades on end.

At this point (at the risk of overstatement and essentialization) the problem I am describing is not simply that which afflicts "Western" industrialized nations or marginalized populations within them, with the church suffering these effects simply because it is "Western."[4] The "Western" church, now located across the globe, suffers isolation in its practices in its own ways and will be the church that I reference most frequently throughout the book. But this is an invitation for Christians globally to do the work of fostering communion: the issue of isolation—and particularly the way it is perpetuated through church practice—is fostered not only through cultural assumptions but also through the common inheritance of Adam.

For the Christian, this is not a surprising finding: sin, as a rupture within created order, ripples outward such that it affects the

---

that churches seek to alleviate this temporary condition, and we neglect the ways in which loneliness depends on a deeper problem: isolation as a theological problem.

4. Marginalized populations experience social isolation in ways unlike "in-groups" of a culture, meaning that they experience isolation in compounded and complex forms. See Matt L. Drabek, *Classify and Label: The Unintended Marginalization of Social Groups* (Lanham, MD: Lexington Books, 2014). Prisoners, for example, suffer in compounded ways, with physical isolation magnifying the emotional and social isolation that comes with the stigma of incarceration. See Lorna A. Rhodes, *Total Confinement: Madness and Reason in Maximum Security Prison* (Berkeley: University of California Press, 2004).

conditions, habits, and practices of human life, with the result that all human life now simply *assumes* the condition of isolation as normal. Having forgotten that sin renders us individuals cut off from one another, culturally, we treat the deeper problem (isolation) as if it were the symptom of the problem (loneliness) or, trying to treat our divided state as a gift, we enhance those elements of culture that celebrate and enable our isolation.

The bad news here is that church practices frequently follow this same pattern. When we're addressing this situation in church, the tendency of late—particularly in Christian literature—is to resource particular kinds of practices that bind people into some kind of community: to draw them in and get them into some form of social activity. But this is to misread the depth of the situation. For even if people begin interacting with one another, the more fundamental problem remains: simply bringing people into association, without duly reflecting on why or how we're doing so, may actually *replicate* isolation. In other words, practices of gathering, without attention to the nature of gathering, run the risk of being constructed in a way that simply assumes isolation as the baseline state, perpetuating the very isolation that is at issue. This conundrum—of isolation, how Christian practices replicate it, and how Christian community is intrinsic to Christ's overcoming of isolation—is what this book addresses.

Beginning Again: Seeing Church Isolation

Cultural isolation and fragmentation is certainly no new topic, having been meditated on by philosophers, historians, cultural critics, and theologians. Most recently, explorations of the deterioration of the common good have taken center stage, and with these explorations a bevy of excellent work targeting specific elements of cultural fragmentation: our obsessions with digital life, the hyperpoliticization of society, and economic division are only a few of the topics explored recently.[5] These proposals are of significant value for

5. Among more recent titles of note are O. Alan Noble, *Disruptive Witness: Speaking Truth in a Distracted Age* (Downers Grove, IL: IVP Academic, 2018); Jay Y. Kim,

relating the church's confessions and Christian theology to the work of social repair. In commending certain practices of repair—whether lessening our distractedness, being good neighbors, paying attention to the world, or speaking justly—writers have (rightly) given a great deal of attention to how Christian goods might serve the reconciling mission of God. Some have offered Christians practices that ground them in a new world for the sake of their neighbors, calling Christians to a renewed ministry of bringing wholeness to a fractured and divided world.

But these excellent proposals neglect, I think, a prior issue: the ways in which isolation affects the ground of these practices, the gathered church. Neglecting this more fundamental question of our life together as the church in favor of practical approaches to addressing social fractures leads to a significant problem: by attending to the practices of the Christian life apart from the assumptions undergirding these practices, the church risks calibrating its practices in a way that amplifies whatever problems are there *internally*. If a church struggles with unacknowledged power issues internally, for example, it risks embodying its evangelism in ways that exemplify power, bringing more agonism into a world already brimming with it. If a church emphasizes the inviolability of the individual, the church can only speak of the practices of the Christian life in ways that magnify individualism and isolation already present culturally. And so Christians must reckon with isolation *within the church*, for if we do not, our addresses to our neighbors will offer new counsels of isolation. The reformation of habit and the rehabilitation of our common life are pressing issues, but we must attend to these in conjunction with the ground out of which our church practices are growing.

The global events of 2020 brought these long-standing concerns about a culture of isolation into focus immediately and clearly. For the better part of the twenty-first century, virtual church was a novelty, and then, for months in 2020, it was a worldwide reality, the only one

---

Analog Church: Why We Need Real People, Places, and Things in the Digital Age (Downers Grove, IL: InterVarsity, 2020); C. Christopher Smith, *How the Body of Christ Talks* (Grand Rapids: Brazos, 2020); and Jake Meador, *In Search of the Common Good: Christian Fidelity in a Fractured World* (Downers Grove, IL: InterVarsity, 2019).

available to millions of Christians spending Sundays at home. It will be nearly impossible to explain this to future generations, how for months the world was shuttered and how gathered churches were the exception. There were no bustling lines to church, no parents slinging children through the door, no groups huddled over donuts or coffee. Isolation, frequently described as manifesting itself "out there" in cultural trends, habits of distraction, and political division, took a physical shape in church in manifold ways, revealing what lay behind our habits of worship and discipleship. We had lived lives for some time now mediated by our technologies, first by email and now by Zoom. We had lived isolated even when in pews together, assuming that there would be others to join our prayers with or voices with. We had selected whom we knew not by who was present to us but by whom we wished to know.

Put differently, one reason that churches were able to glide with relative ease into a season of social distancing and isolation was that, as churches, we had been *trained to be isolated for years*. What was operationally true in our church practice had been exposed. And in the wake of this exposure, an opportunity has appeared: to examine the ways in which the church contributed to isolation and continues to do so. But with the exposure of a problem, here, too, we are offered an opportunity to hear something true: this emaciated form of relating to one another is not who we have been given in Christ to be.

Dietrich Bonhoeffer as Guide

Vexing questions call for able guides, and so it is to Dietrich Bonhoeffer we will primarily turn, for two reasons. First, Bonhoeffer's many discussions of church life are not, as many contemporary works on church life are, practical guides to building Christian community, helpful hints for building community groups. Bonhoeffer invites us to a kind of theological therapy, an invitation to unlearn our practices of isolation that we have, over time, calibrated our church gatherings and practices to. We are invited not to acquire a set of habits for the sake of our improvement but to participate in the healing, through these habits, of our deeper wound of isolation from one another and from

God. Second, his work offers an account of the Christian community that seeks its own healing in tandem with the world's healing; it is not a matter of withdrawal from a fragmented world that is offered so much as a journey *into* the world's fragmentation, so that we might learn what difference the body of Christ makes and so that we might gather up the fragments of the world as we go into it.

In other words, our predicament is not first a failure of imagination about our corporate lives but rather a failure of habituation: we cannot think or imagine our way out of the isolation that is the mark of sin so much as pray, eat, sing, and serve our way out. When we hold up our practices to the vision that Bonhoeffer presents, his images can seem impossible or unrealistic, but this is, I think, only because the presumption of sin's isolation has so deeply wrapped itself around our imagination, our assumptions about the moral life, and our collective practices that we cannot imagine a different world than one of isolation. In *The Emergence of Sin*, Matthew Croasmun helpfully explicates how cultural patterns of sin reflect and shape the wills of the ones who sin; this notion of sin as shaping us helps us to name how church cultures of isolation are born out of—and shape—the ways in which we view the gift of Christians gathering together in deficient and limited ways. When we inhabit and practice a church culture shaped by isolation long enough, it becomes the only way that seems thinkable to us.[6]

Over the next seven chapters, we will enter into a prolonged discussion to provide a vision of both what we have lost in the practice of being church and what we might yet regain. Bonhoeffer, best known for being the pastor who resisted the Nazis in Germany, was above all things a theologian who found himself building a seminary out of limited resources, training dissenting seminarians who wanted to help rebuild a failing and apostate church. It was during this time that he too found himself driven to ask what moored and enlivened the church as a living body of Christ.[7] Many elements of

6. Matthew Croasmun, *The Emergence of Sin: The Cosmic Tyrant in Romans* (Oxford: Oxford University Press, 2019).

7. For a provocative read of Bonhoeffer as a theologian living in cultural collapse, see Andrew DeCort, *Bonhoeffer's New Beginning: Ethics after Devastation* (Minneapolis: Fortress, 2018).

church life, such as the long-standing arrangement of state support for ministerial training and church pensions, still operated during the Second World War. But many of the understood arrangements of the relationship of church to state began to come undone.[8] It was not as if this was the first time that there had been a community of Christians living together in the shambles of a church. But for Bonhoeffer, it was the occasion for offering a therapy for a church seeking renewal in the midst of cultural catastrophe, for the church had drunk from the same cultural, ideological, and theological wells as the state and was likewise in need of healing.

The extreme case of Nazi Germany is built on this mundane point: our shared life as churches is, though hidden in Christ, not immune from the conditions of creaturely life, sustained only by the "spiritual."[9] If our being gathered together as the church is a gathering that takes seriously the earthbound nature of human life, and if it is as humans that we are knit together by God's own Spirit, then the church is the most fragile of creatures—not in spite of God's work, but because of it. For Christ does not lift us beyond creation, but the Spirit unites us as the church as children of dust, through the habits of being God's creatures.

This is not, as it were, a "Bonhoeffer book": Bonhoeffer is one of the key guides to helping us diagnose the ways in which church practice perpetuates the isolation common to creation, and we will engage at

8. It is part of the hagiography surrounding Bonhoeffer's legacy that obscures us from seeing the ways in which real structural and procedural forces within the German Evangelical Church contributed both to the Confessing Church's emergence and to its subsequent failure. For background on these bureaucratic arrangements that contributed to the Confessing Church's failure, see Christiane Tietz, *Theologian of Reality: The Life and Thought of Dietrich Bonhoeffer* (Minneapolis: Fortress, 2016), 35–77; and Victoria Barnett, *For the Soul of the People: Protestant Protest against Hitler* (New York: Oxford University Press, 1992).

9. Andrew Davison, *Why Sacraments?* (London: SPCK, 2013), 9: "The Christian tradition will not let the 'spiritual' be simply spiritual or the 'material' be simply material. It shows this by constantly taking material things and dragging them into church . . . and by constantly taking spiritual things and enacting them materially. This does not *create* an entanglement between the spiritual and the material; it recognizes one that already exists. Friedrich Schelling (1775–1854) saw that the spiritual, when only 'spiritual,' is banal, even evil: 'Evil is in a certain respect completely spiritual, for it carries on the most emphatic war against all being, indeed it would like to negate the ground of creation.'"

length with the themes, insights, and scholarship surrounding him. But it offers no overarching account of how Bonhoeffer ought to be read on any number of finer points. Bonhoeffer remains one of the most contested figures in Christian theology,[10] and disagreements over how to best interpret him will continue for some time. My concern here is primarily to assess the ways in which Bonhoeffer's vision of church-community provides wisdom for contemporary church practice.

But more importantly, this is a book that is not directly about Bonhoeffer but about one of the things that Bonhoeffer cared most about: the church and its witness. Along the way, I indicate those places where Bonhoeffer's concerns and my own diverge and those places where I outrun the specific concerns of Bonhoeffer's writing. His work, in sum, is employed here as one employs a map: to provide orientation and illumination for the larger contours of the land at stake, that as we travel the terrain in practice, we might understand how to better walk it.

The Road Ahead

In chapter 1, we will explore the nature of isolation and of Christian communion, to clarify what it means to say that the church is not only Christ's body in creation but also Christ's body *gathered in* creation. Coming to terms with this is essential because in seeing the church as birthed by the Spirit but dwelling in and through the earth, we can come to terms with how the isolation common to creation comes to dwell within the body of the church. Chapter 2 continues this work as we come to terms with the fact that the isolation we inherit by virtue of being created and fallen human beings is frequently replicated in and through church practices, both liturgical and technological. When the church operates independent of a thoroughgoing vision of the church as a body meant for communion with God, these practices and technologies (at their best) offer only a foreshortened vision that might mitigate some aspects of isolation, such as staving off loneliness, providing content to congregants weary from the week's labors,

10. For this, see Stephen R. Haynes, *The Bonhoeffer Phenomenon: Portraits of a Protestant Saint* (Minneapolis: Fortress, 2004).

or offering a respite from cultural isolation. But at their worst, these practices replicate the isolation they were meant to undo, allowing the church to assume isolation as the condition that churches must mimic if we are to be faithful witnesses within creation.

In chapter 3 we will begin to cast a vision of the church as communion, in need of healing from its isolation. This is in part an act of mourning, for it requires recognizing that frequently what we have used to hold us together, even in our physical presence to one another, is not Christ. It is only when we mourn our losses and allow that mourning to penetrate down through the good memories of the past that we can begin the hard work: practicing communion and inviting Christ to undo our state of isolation.

Describing the therapy—coming to terms with how isolation is unmade and charting a way forward—will occupy the remainder of the book. Chapter 4 turns our attention to the practices of the gathered church, of worship and communion, to ask not only *what* we do but *how* we do it if in fact church practice is about being knit into one body in Christ and overcoming the isolation that is regnant in creation. Chapter 5 turns us away from the time of gathering and toward how this shapes our scattering into the world. The habitual nature of these gathered church practices of "the day together," as Bonhoeffer terms it in *Life Together*, sets the tone for "the day apart," the time when we are scattered into the world in ordinary life. This chapter will thus describe the spiritual practices of the days we spend apart from the gathered church, showing how the practices—both in what we do and *how* we do it—are meant to extend the internal work of the gathered church into the folds of life when Christians scatter into the world.

One of the dire temptations of our ordinary life is to see what happens in church as extraordinary, performed under more ideal conditions, such that our life of piety in the world is a matter of endurance at best and accommodation at worst to the terms set by isolation. But the form of prayer, the forms of speech, and the practices of Scripture of these days cohere to the priorities of what is communicated when the church gathers, so that the scattered church does not operate always bouncing between poles of communion when gathered and isolation when apart, but instead views its days apart as ordered back toward corporate gatherings.

Having offered a way to envision the practices of the Christian community when it is gathered and scattered as one coherent whole ordered toward the undoing of isolation, in chapter 6, I will help us to marry the spiritual practices of the Christian life to the ordinary practices and habits that characterize both Christian liturgy and the ordinary lives of Christians together. Speech, admonition, listening, mutual aid, and bearing of burdens are described as those practices that continue to reshape our lives away from a presumption of isolation and toward a presumption of belonging together in communion before God.[11] And so, the final chapter, chapter 7, turns to the culminating practices of confession and Communion, in which we see most clearly the communion with God that the church is meant for. The practices of the church—listening, Scripture reading, prayer, and so forth—prepare participants to recognize themselves as unified as one body, with mutual confession and Communion being the capstone of previous practices and also being those practices that deepen the others.

What is sought in these pages is not an idealized community immune from sin or free from the isolating forces of creation. What is sought here is a vision of the body of Christ that emerges as a community, a community through which the world might be knit together. In Christ we are called to be those who are done with isolation's tyranny, though during our time in this world, isolation may never be fully done with us. And so, as we recover a vision of the church appropriate to this calling, I hope we learn to be those who embrace the kingdom that has come as the light in the darkness, even if the darkness remains perplexed by the communion that the kingdom brings in the midst of a normalized isolation.

---

11. As Tom Greggs puts it, "The divine gift of community in the church, through an act of the Spirit, is a reversing by grace of the fall and its effects" (*The Breadth of Salvation: Rediscovering the Fullness of God's Saving Work* [Grand Rapids: Baker Academic, 2020], 38). See also Greggs, *Dogmatic Ecclesiology*, vol. 1, *The Priestly Catholicity of the Church* (Grand Rapids: Baker Academic, 2019), 99: "To be filled with the Spirit and thereby to share in the true humanity of Christ is to be opened up toward the other. It is to see one's own identity as bound with the other in Christ at a more fundamental level than individual identities." It is not that there is a sequential order—that one gets things right with Christ and then one's neighbor—but rather a contemporaneity of the two: we are joined to Christ *as* we embrace the communion that is given to us with one another in Christ, with our neighbors.

PART ONE

ISOLATION AND THE STRUCTURE OF THE WORLD

One

Life in Isolation, Then and Now

Isolation Everywhere, Everywhere Invisible

Among the most bone-chilling moments in the Bible is the story of Jesus in the garden of Gethsemane, in which we find Jesus—just days removed from the adulation of the crowds—telling his disciples that he is "deeply grieved, even to death" (Mark 14:34). The narrative occasion of this grief is Jesus's impending arrest and crucifixion, but it is accompanied at all points with an increasing isolation from his disciples, from his family, and from the public. These emotional afflictions of Jesus, we are reminded, are not shadow play: Jesus encounters the reality of creaturely life that is isolation and sin.[1] For as Jesus prayed, his disciples slept, and as Jesus died on the cross, he was

---

1. Maximus the Confessor, "Opusculum 6: On the Two Wills of Christ in the Agony of Gethsemane," in *On the Cosmic Mystery of Jesus Christ*, trans. Paul M. Blowers (Crestwood, NY: St. Vladimir's Seminary Press, 2003). Maximus rightly contends that Christ, being one with the Father, cannot be separated from the Father. But this does not preclude the human passions of Christ being afflicted: Paul Blowers rightly notes that Maximus affirms Christ's fear of death as a sign of his true humanity, "aimed ultimately at modeling self-abnegation and emboldening those who confront death on the basis of their obedience" (176).

yet surrounded. When Jesus enters Gethsemane, as his disciples fall asleep both physically and metaphorically, we see him weighed down by the existential condition of being a creature in the fallen world: bearing an isolation and fear common to humanity's condition.

In this scene in the garden we see Christ bearing our creaturely condition and mending it. The Son who could never be separate from Father or Holy Spirit is, in his flesh, bearing the isolation of humanity. The agony of Gethsemane was not, as some modern interpreters would describe it, the triune God being divided or undergoing abandonment within the triune God. Rather, Christ was, as William Stringfellow would describe it, confronting one of the many emissaries of Death—the persistent reminder that we are frail creatures of dust and will die.[2] In this encounter of Christ in the garden, we see that isolation is a theological problem before it is a social one. Being isolated is more than being lonely, for in companionship we find a temporary reprieve; isolation—the condition of being structurally, morally, and spiritually estranged within creation—is a more pervasive theological condition in which a person finds themselves cut off even when surrounded by people.

To say that many modern societies are fundamentally individualistic—built on the premise that you qua you should actualize the fullness of your individuality—is nothing new: this much historians, philosophers, theologians, and cultural critics have been pointing out for years.[3] When it is built into structures of advertising, politics, and cultural engagement, this individualism creates cultures in which the cultivated individual—apart from other social bodies—becomes the ideal and, further, comes to believe that social structures that

2. William Stringfellow, *A Keeper of the Word: Selected Writings of William Stringfellow* (Grand Rapids: Eerdmans, 1994), 199: "In the Fall, every human being, every principality, everything exists in a condition of estrangement from its own life, as well as from the lives of all other human beings, powers and things."

3. Charles Taylor, *The Malaise of Modernity* (Toronto: House of Anansi Press, 1998), and Zygmunt Bauman, *Liquid Times: Living in an Age of Uncertainty* (New York: Polity, 2006), point to the ways in which the individualist presupposition—that a person should be self-authenticating—has led to the loss of social institutions capable of supporting our quests for freedom. Likewise, Francis Fukuyama, *Identity: The Demand for Dignity and the Politics of Resentment* (New York: Farrar, Straus & Giroux, 2018), demonstrates that, once individualism becomes the presupposition, further political fragmentation is to be expected.

limit this must be removed. This presumption, that we are isolated from one another and must make the best of this, surrounds us both philosophically and culturally: we find it in children's programming,[4] hardwired into the design framework of smartphones,[5] and bundled into how we think about disease recovery.[6] Once imbibed as a cultural value, this presumption propagates to the point that thinking of a unifying "culture" comes to seem novel, and it has birthed a thousand think pieces on mending social isolation and fragmentation.

How creation emerges out of this problem is not first a question of political societies, one that could be resolved by a nationalist program on the one hand (shoring up our common social identity) or by resorting to a cosmopolitan vision on the other (expanding our economic and political relationships to the whole of the world). For the Christian, human union is restored not solely by acts of political solidarity but by coming together in Christ. This human union that we receive in Christ is exemplified in the body of Christ, in whom enemies are reconciled and opposing fragments of the world are knit together, with what we are as the church becoming the basis for our life amid our neighbors.

As Bonhoeffer writes, the proposal of "solidarity," either theologically or politically conceived, provides, ironically, too *weak* a basis for the restoration of communion; what we need is not to be joined in our isolation but to be healed:[7] "To bring this about, Jesus

4. Melinda Aley, Lindsay Hahn, Ron Tamborini, Henry Goble, Lu Zhang, Sara M. Grady, and Joshua Baldwin, "The Representation of Altruistic and Egoistic Motivations in Children's TV Programming," *Communication Research Reports* 34 (2017): 58–67.

5. Michelle Cleary, Sancia West, and Denis Visentin, "The Mental Health Impacts of Smartphone and Social Media Use," *Mental Health Psychosocial Factors* 41 (2020): 755–57. As we see in a recent study by Brian A. Primack, Sabrina A. Karim, Ariel Shensa, Nicholas Bowman, Jennifer Knight, and Jamie E. Sidani, "Positive and Negative Experiences on Social Media and Perceived Social Isolation," *American Journal of Health Promotion* 33 (2019): 859–68, some of these negative effects correlate to expectations of negativity concerning social media use. A (negative) narrative account of the effects of smartphones and social media on the structure of social interactions can be found in Sherry Turkle, *Alone Together: Why We Expect More from Technology and Less from Each Other* (New York: Basic Books, 2011).

6. Giada Danesi, Celine Bourquin, Friedrich Stiefel, Khalil Zaman, and Michael Saraga, "The Isolation of Cancer Survivors," *European Journal of Cancer Care* 29, no. 2, https://onlinelibrary.wiley.com/doi/full/10.1111/ecc.13194.

7. Dietrich Bonhoeffer, *Sanctorum Communio: A Theological Study of the Sociology of the Church*, trans. Reinhard Krauss and Nancy Lukens, Dietrich

calls to repentance, which means he reveals God's ultimate claim and subjects the human past and present to its reality. Recognizing that we are guilty makes us solitary before God; we begin to recognize what has long been the case objectively, namely that we are in a state of isolation."[8]

The irony here is that solidarity offers an important, but limited, sense of union, for solidarity stands with and joins cause with the one who is broken and oppressed but yet stands separate from them, producing in turn new political alternatives that are themselves organized around this principle of isolation but never communion.[9] In solidarity, I offer myself to another but cannot fully share with their state, for their oppression can never be identical with my oppression: I may advocate for them and bear witness for them, but I remain divided from their experience of suffering. Solidarity enters into a relationship of advocacy with others but assumes the division of the suffering and the advocate as the basis for the relationship. For Bonhoeffer, God comes to us *in and through* the very creaturely life in which we operate as isolated beings, offering a vision beyond solidarity: "Thus out of utter isolation arises concrete community, for the preaching of God's love speaks of the community into which God *has* entered with each and every person—with all those who in utter solitude know themselves separated from God and other

---

Bonhoeffer Works 1 (Minneapolis: Fortress, 1996), 148: "By placing himself within this community-of-Israel, Christ does not declare his solidarity with it, but in vicarious representative action for all he fulfills the law by love."

8. Bonhoeffer, *Sanctorum Communio*, 149.

9. This is not to say that "solidarity," as either a theological or political concept, is not useful or necessary, but only that it operates out of a limited anthropology. As Rebecca Todd Peters describes it in *Solidarity Ethics: Transformation in a Globalized World* (Minneapolis: Fortress, 2014), 51, "Solidarity describes a state of being in which two or more distinct communities or groups of people develop a bond or a relationship based on a shared interest, value or goal," rooted in the vision in Genesis 1–2 of creation in communion and lived out in these shared goals and interests. While emphasizing the importance of this advocacy, we must note that the relation established across communities then becomes one of shared action and interest built on a commitment to difference and a recognition of the dangers of hegemonic unity. What emerges here is an anthropological vision in which groups of people—committed internally to difference and union through shared goals—are united by shared external actions that emphasize distance between persons and mediate that distance by common goals. In Bonhoeffer's terminology, this is not a community but a crowd.

human beings and who believe this message."[10] The undoing of our fractured, divided state of sin occurs hand in hand with being given a new community in which all people are knit together with one another in a very different fashion: the community of the church, Christ's own body.

In his work on theological education, Willie James Jennings highlights the difficulties of this defragmenting work, particularly for theological communities: in seeking to create whole persons, we ignore the reality of the fragments that we *are*—fragmentation is not simply something we live amid, but our very state. In training ministers, Jennings argues, we double down on the becoming whole without first contending with the fact that "we creatures live in pieces, and we come to know our redemption in pieces."[11] As Jennings argues, the fragmentation of our world—shaped by the manifold powers of race, money, and colonialization—has left the Western world with the illusion of wholeness, but it is a wholeness that Christians have only by displacing that fragmentation on others.

Here, we must ask questions: What happens when "church" is, as Jennings suggests, largely a mirror of social isolation, not an alternative to it? Returning to the image of Jesus in the garden, surrounded by sleeping disciples, we see that this is to be expected: the church does not remain indefectible as some perfect body of practice, never retreating from its vocation to be the body of Christ in the world. As we saw in the introduction, creation is given as a common gift in which the City of God and the Earthly City are intertwined. While,

10. Bonhoeffer, *Sanctorum Communio*, 149.

11. Willie James Jennings, *After Whiteness: An Education in Belonging* (Grand Rapids: Eerdmans, 2021), 34. Adoption of traditions as a means to escape this fragmentation dissolves the person into a perceived unity, often in an arbitrary fashion. In other words, fragmentation is not escaped by adopting purely external solutions. As Jennings writes, "It could be that forming people in ecclesial traditions and the Christian tradition more broadly is the best way to imagine theological education, but until we wrestle with the man lurking inside a tradition, performing himself in the quest for a maturity that has been presented to theological education, . . . we will lock students in a formation that will take much more than it will give and that will deny us all the gift of working with the fragments" (46). As will become more clear, I agree with Jennings about the frequently superficial ways in which tradition is adopted as an antidote to the fragmentation of the world, and I will register my disagreements later.

positively, this intermixing provides points of contact for witness to the world, so that the world might be drawn into the City of God and be saved, this state of *permixtum* also means that the church will bear the scars of sin common to creation. It is to the ways in which isolation occurs in our church practice that we must turn our gaze.

Church and Regnant Isolation

It remains true, though not without some hyperbole, that the church is the alternative to the world.[12] But the key difficulty with naming the church as the embodied alternative to a world beyond the isolation that is the mark of sin is that, in most churches, isolation remains a regnant assumption of how churches work. That is, in many cases, churches are organized not as a community in opposition to isolation but as an organization that amplifies it. The gifts we bring to the church, including the gifts of ourselves and our time, all bear the marks from the time we spend in the world, our minds and bodies conformed to the logics of isolation, our loves forged by Mammon's many lingering shadows. Saying that what churches do replicates the isolation of the world is not a judgment on our church life so much as it is an acknowledgment that our ways of church bear out the mixed quality of living during time.[13]

To see how churches do this in practice, we must consider the inner relationship between two social phenomena: crowds and individuals. On the surface, these seem different both in nature and scope.

12. Most famous for this sentiment is Stanley Hauerwas, who has made this claim in one form or another on multiple occasions, as in *A Community of Character: Toward a Constructive Christian Social Ethic* (Notre Dame, IN: University of Notre Dame Press, 1981), 108: "The church in its profoundest expression is the gathering of a people who are able to sustain one another throughout the inevitable tragedies of our lives. They are able to do so because they have been formed by a narrative, constantly reenacted through the sharing of a meal, that claims nothing less than that God has taken the tragic character of our existence into his very life."

13. Charles Mathewes's account of the *permixtum*, the temporal entanglement between church and world, is illuminating here, emphasizing the ways in which the virtues of being the church in time are those that embrace the entangled relationship of the "two cities" (of God and of the world), pushing the church past "dialogue" and toward a "proleptic communion." *A Theology of Public Life* (Cambridge: Cambridge University Press, 2007), 105–42.

Individuals theologically would seem to be in danger of neglecting the gathered assembly, of forgetting the ways in which friendship forms us as moral beings, while crowds are the un-isolation, the large gathering that doubles down on the presence of other people. But scratching the surface reveals their commonality. If I go to a Black Friday sale, I am there for the sole purpose of getting a great deal on an otherwise overpriced good, and I'd just as soon the other people *not* be there. In a crowd, the group exists as a group of individuals who are only accidentally related to one another.[14] When we begin to examine our church practice in this way, we see that frequently our practices do not attend to isolation but simply aggregate it and then perpetuate it in new ways.

In the next chapter, we will unearth this more carefully, but once we see this relationship between the isolated individual and the crowd, we see that this ethos is embedded everywhere in church:

- It is Communion that we were able to conduct virtually, because we think of the bread and cup as having only individual meaning and doled out in individual portions.
- It is the singing we optionally participate in, in response to a band or choir that does the work for the congregation.
- It is the sermon pitched toward personal application and making meaning out of our preexisting lives, lives that are ours to craft and live.
- It is the Bible study whose meaning, pedagogically, depends on our personal ideas, assessments of truthfulness, and individual applications of that meaning.
- It is a doctrine of justification that treats salvation as that which depends on the agency of the individual.
- It is a view of conscience that requires the believer to make unlimited assessment of the truthfulness or falsehood of doctrines and morals.

14. Bonhoeffer, *Sanctorum Communio*, 93–94: "In the mass there is no genuine social bonding of wills; instead wills are seen as mechanical forces reacting to stimuli, so to speak. . . . In the mass, the boundary of personhood is lost, and the individual is no longer a person but only a part of the mass, drawn into and directed by it."

With these kinds of activities, even when gathered under the sign of the crowd, the individual is being habituated to know what they are as a sole individual before God, unmediated and unattached. This vision of what we are is, of course, erroneous. As Rowan Williams reminds us, this differentiation and individual agency depend on a shared world in which language, common understandings of nature, and communications of all kinds are possible: it is the abundance of what we share that makes it possible for us to even begin to think that all the riches we have as persons belong solely to the individual.[15] But much of our practice as church operates contrary to Williams's insight. And so, if the gospel was only ever about me becoming more of an individual, then the gathered church was only ever a crowd, a group of individuals. And if what the church is can, without remainder, be delivered to the individual, why now do I need to gather at all?

As we shall see shortly, the isolation that church frequently replicates is one with which we are deeply acquainted, one that is *habitual* and deeply ingrained within us, a mark of the sin that has ruptured our world. Charles Taylor's thesis about modern persons as "buffered," isolated individuals who are unaccountable to one another—true self-created individuals—provides us some clarity from a historical vantage point, but the larger theological claim here is that isolation is part and parcel of the ground out of which human society has been growing since nearly the beginning.[16] This impulse toward fragmentation and isolation has had a certain way of appearing since the late Middle Ages, and scholars such as Taylor are right to point us to these ways in which we continue to manifest it. But this isolation, as I have been arguing so far, is an old story,

15. Rowan Williams, *Lost Icons: Reflections on Cultural Bereavement* (Harrisburg, PA: Morehouse Publishing, 2000), 58. One is reminded of the parable of the prodigal (Luke 15:11–32), in which the prodigal's journey away from the father occurs solely because of the money given to him by the father; Bonhoeffer develops this line of interpretation in *Sanctorum Communio*, 69–70.

16. For Taylor's work on this question, see in particular *A Secular Age* (Cambridge, MA: Belknap, 2007); and *Sources of the Self: The Making of the Modern Identity* (Cambridge, MA: Harvard University Press, 1992). For guidance on the implications of Taylor's work for Christian discipleship, see Andrew Root, *Faith Formation in a Secular Age: Responding to the Church's Obsession with Youthfulness* (Grand Rapids: Baker Academic, 2017).

predating the modern age, and not one recently learned: both those who retreat from the crowds *and* those in the faceless crowd are part of the same phenomenon. Both the religious renegade and the religious conformist—both the one engaged in religious bricolage and the member of the crowded auditorium—are shaped and moved by a deeper commonality: isolation. To see how it is that this isolation exists in such contradictory forms—and what it means for churches to unlearn the habits of isolation that are so deeply ingrained within us—let us turn to our guide, Dietrich Bonhoeffer.

The Origins of Isolation

In the beginning of his lectures on the first three chapters of Genesis, Bonhoeffer makes an astute observation: we have a sense, almost intuitive to us, that we are meant to be free, though we have no way, by reason, to account for where it comes from or, frequently, what to do with it.[17] Bonhoeffer writes that, despite our attempts to orient ourselves within creation—to find ground beneath our feet—

> humankind no longer lives in the beginning; instead it has lost the beginning. Now it finds itself in the middle, knowing neither the end nor the beginning, and yet knowing that it is in the middle. It knows therefore that it comes from the beginning and must move on toward the end. It sees its life as determined by these two factors, concerning which it knows only that it does not know them. . . . Humankind knows itself to be totally deprived of its own self-determination, because it comes from the beginning and is moving toward the end without knowing what that means.[18]

Put succinctly, we all come into a world that exists under the sign of the wandering Cain, preserved by God and yet alone. The beginning that has been lost is God, the one in whom our orientation within

17. Here Bonhoeffer has in mind specifically the accounts of Hegel in which there is infinite freedom, whose starting point Hegel attempts to secure with an account of reason. Dietrich Bonhoeffer, *Creation and Fall: A Theological Exposition of Genesis 1–3*, trans. Douglas Stephen Bax, Dietrich Bonhoeffer Works 3 (Minneapolis: Fortress, 1997), 27.

18. Bonhoeffer, *Creation and Fall*, 28.

time consists.[19] There is no going back and understanding our own
beginning apart from having it mediated to us by God: we cannot
discover it for ourselves but only receive it from God as a gift.[20] Humanity desired freedom from the limiting gifts of God and from the
life-giving responsibilities toward one another, and we were given
what we asked for.

The irony of this freedom is that, like Adam and Eve in their procession from the garden, we attempt to carve out a firm standpoint
together in creation, a stance from which to orient ourselves, only
to find that our positioning of ourselves divides us further from one
another. We discover to our horror that we are all inheritors of the
original sin insofar as we repeat this "unending burden" in ways
unique to our time and place. Writing, "The guilt is mine alone: I
have committed evil in the midst of the original state of creation,"
Bonhoeffer offers a picture of participatory guilt: modern humans
are not the hapless inheritors of another's guilt but willingly repeat
the sins of our predecessors, creating new and novel forms of division and isolation.[21]

In Bonhoeffer's meditation here, we find that God's intent in
giving humans this world to live in was that we would be mediated
together by God, with God and one another: a life of communion.
Even with the first two persons, the design was not *unmediated*
existence, but that the man and the woman were brought together
in God, their limits of body being the very vehicle by which they
could be in communion with one another. Their ability to call one
another "flesh of my flesh" assumed that the flesh they shared was a
borrowed good, built off of borrowed breath and living in a borrowed

19. Bonhoeffer has little interest in questions of human origins as construed in
the creationist debates. For him, the question of how to position ourselves in time
has less to do with knowing the nature of the universe's origins and much more to
do with knowing the God who has created the universe. To be preoccupied with the
universe's origins in order to live well is for Bonhoeffer part of the problem, not the
solution, for such an approach attempts to secure our identity and orientation for
life according to rational inquiry instead of receiving the world as the gift of God
and our place within it as within that economy.

20. Bonhoeffer, *Creation and Fall*, 30.

21. Bonhoeffer, *Creation and Fall*, 105. To my earlier point about Taylor, modernity breaks human life in novel ways, but isolation is not simply a product of
modernity or curable by adopting premodern habits.

earth: to be God's creatures was to disavow autonomy, self-creation, and even immediate access to another. We can no more make an immediate claim of possession on one another than we could make such a claim on the earth from which we came. In other words, there was no time in which we could know either God *or one another* without mediation: our very ability to be human depended not on our authenticity but on our entanglement with one another, an entanglement that we find ourselves in but cannot claim to be the originators or possessors of.

Consider the placement of the tree of life, Bonhoeffer observes: it exists not at the edge of the garden—as if it were something in addition to a sustainable or coherent human life—but at the very center. At the very center of the most intimate account of God's relation to humanity, there is a limit: we remain able to be human, together, only to the degree that we remain dependent on the One who is beyond us. We are prohibited from eating the tree of knowledge for the same reason: in refusing to eat from that tree, we are embracing the limits and contingency of being human, and thus we receive the gift of being bound to one another and to God instead of having the resources to make and remake ourselves absolutely.[22]

This vision may seem alien to us, for we intuitively think of our most intimate human relations as *not* needing mediation: the more immediately present to one another the better. But, as Bonhoeffer argues, this assumption is a product of the fall. For once we assume that we do not need to have our lives together *mediated*, we begin to become architects of the world. Our vision of the self becomes centralized, and we envision society as a matter of Archimedean planning, looking for a place in which we can leverage our vision of the world from aspiration into reality. In doing so, we construct a world without God, with others only as *accidentally* there: they are not necessary to me being me, any more than they need me to become themselves. Humans exchange this contingency and mediation, this communion with one another rooted in God, for knowledge and immediacy. The trade they make is one of trust for self-making, creating new forms of common life that must always be cultivated and always

22. Bonhoeffer, *Creation and Fall*, 84–85.

be defended because it is constantly now our vocation to create our lives together from the ground up, a parody of creation ex nihilo.[23]

Before the fall, when life was given and existence was a gift, others were co-inheritors of the gift, those whose presence was not competitive: there was always enough to go around because the source of our life—God—is endless. In the old world, we saw each other in gratitude, as cosharers and partners. In the other person, we saw not a competitor but a living vision of the limit that is intrinsic to creation: in the same way that there is a limit to being human, so the other person was a gracious limit that I loved and knew as a gift.

After the fall, we lose the sense of being mediated by God to others, and others appear to us as a limit to our power and agency. Now—since we are condemned to live and build ourselves anew—the presence and limits imposed by the will of another person are only a challenge to us: "A person then desires only, in an unbounded way, to possess the other or to destroy the other. For now the human being insists on that human being's own contribution to, and claim upon, the other, insists that the other is derived from oneself; what the human being until now accepted humbly at this point becomes a cause for pride and rebellion. *That is our world.*"[24]

Having refused to be limited, we find that others become competitors—within families, within friendships, within cities. And this then drives us to be alone, for it is only in being alone that we alone can be the judges of our conscience, of our actions, of our needs, and of our lives. It is only by being separated from everyone—even God—that we think we can fully live as humans in this new world of our own making.[25] Whether we live into this new reality of the war of all against all by trying to overcome it heroically or by retreating into the safety of a tribe, these are—as we have seen—only mirror responses to the same condition of isolation. As Bonhoeffer insightfully points out, in a world of sin, this clinging to another to alleviate this condition of isolation is not community but a form of *hiding*, trying to escape the division from God and from others through escaping into a crowd or by creating a world in our own image.

23. Bonhoeffer, *Creation and Fall*, 91.
24. Bonhoeffer, *Creation and Fall*, 99 (emphasis added).
25. Bonhoeffer, *Creation and Fall*, 128–36.

This response to our condition, which we see first in the response of Adam to God, permeates many of our responses to the isolation of sin now: "Adam in fleeing must realize that he cannot escape from his Creator. We have all had the dream in which we want to flee from something horrible and yet cannot flee from it. . . . The same thing is now expressed in Adam's answer: I am naked and so I hid myself. . . . He tries to flee further and yet knows that he has already been apprehended. I am sinful, I cannot stand before you. Just because you are a sinner, stand before me and do not flee."[26] Rather than accept the hard word about who we are and, in hearing it, be saved from our autonomy, we simply seek to hide physically, emotionally, spiritually, relationally either by separating from others or by losing ourselves in a crowd.

This impulse to seek safety from this state is precisely the impulse people have after they realize they are fragmented from one another: hiding.[27] And since then, we have invented elaborate ways to facilitate that hiding, even in religious circles. Sometimes we call it the inviolability of conscience; sometimes we call it a refusal to feel shame; sometimes it's an insistence on seeing ourselves as the full measure of our moral wisdom and behavior or the evasion of the scrutiny of the kind questions of others about our situations.[28] And so, even when I seek out the company of others, because I am fundamentally alone, such alliances are inevitably short-lived: you may be a help now, but you may be my competitor later. If I do seek your company, it is only because you shelter me from having to face myself.

To describe our existence in sin in terms of isolation yields a complex character of our condition. Following the description of Genesis, the physical forms of our gatherings are shaped by this prior theological reality, as isolation moves from simply being an interpersonal reality to being a social and creation-wide reality. As Genesis unfolds, we are treated to a vision of this movement, as the isolation between Adam, Eve, and God unfolds into a presumption that implicates their

26. Bonhoeffer, *Creation and Fall*, 129.
27. Bonhoeffer, *Creation and Fall*, 128–29. In Genesis, when God returns to the garden after the humans have disobeyed, God has to call out to them, for it has become their first instinct to hide from God and to conceal themselves.
28. Bonhoeffer, *Creation and Fall*, 128.

offspring and, ultimately, the entire earth. In the years after the flood, too, humanity attempts to stave off the uncertainty and fragility of their calling out into the world, to repopulate the earth, by clinging to one another in a city designed to facilitate their collective hiding from God. In the same way, then, the world we design mirrors our isolation, perpetuating it without our conscious response, reaffirming this primal logic.

The responses of Adam and Eve (accusing one another and hiding in the trees) are, in the end, two sides of the same coin: responses to a world in which we are divided from one another. Their positioning of themselves over against one another in an attempt to gain footing and their retreat from the presence of others are, in the end, two ways of responding to our condition of isolation under sin. Once we see this, the ways in which this core of isolation radiates out into the world become clearer and clearer. Isolation is evident not only in the one who cannot bear being alone; it also appears in the one who exalts themselves and their desires over against others, unable to bear the true presence of difference. It is the family that withdraws from any criticism of their family habits *and* the family that succumbs to every social pressure to conform. It is both the nation that pulls out of all arrangements into seclusion from the world *and* the nation that refuses responsibility by hiding amid a company of other nations. Overcoming isolation either by pulling away and disappearing or by agonistic defiance of the claims of others are two faces of the same problem.

Structures of social isolation both compound and are shaped by relational isolation. As Adam and Eve left the garden, their spiritual isolation from God was of a piece with their relational isolation from one another—Adam no longer considered Eve "flesh of my flesh" but "this woman whom you gave to be with me" (Gen. 2:23; 3:12).[29] Our isolation, embedded in relational presumptions and habits and codified into laws and policies, reinforces, in private and public forms,

29. Brian Bantum has helpfully extended this insight to the ways in which bodies are named in differentiated fashion, an indicator of the fall in our attempts to name, classify, and organize raced bodies in ways that create division in the image of the one who makes the classifications. *The Death of Race* (Minneapolis: Fortress, 2016), 45–52.

an isolation from one another that now emerges as the only thinkable option. For Bonhoeffer, we encounter all of these different facets of isolation—the interpersonal, the political, the private, and even the churchly—as an intertwined phenomenon, such that this nexus cannot be undone except by addressing the whole. When Bonhoeffer, writing about the fall, says "that is our world," he is offering a way for the reader to understand how the dynamics and actions of Genesis are not something that happened once upon a time but a description of how sin repeatedly breaks the world.

As mentioned previously with the work of Charles Taylor, the *ways* in which people learn to be individuals and embrace isolation have changed under modernity, but theologically, the fundamental problem has remained the same. Isolation will present itself differently in a society that is individualistic, but this is not to say that in previous eras isolation was not already at work in differentiated ways—in the stratification of society into castes and classes, in the tyrannies of Rome where the good of the caesar was the good that mattered, in the xenophobias of both East and West. Humans are incredibly inventive at breaking themselves in novel ways, though the animating principle remains common.

But Why Community?

If, as Bonhoeffer suggests, isolation is not simply a physical state that can be pressed on us but something humans do almost by habit *as sinners*, then two things are true. First, "church as gathered body" is an insufficient response to this. If "isolation" is not merely a physical but a *theological* phenomenon, then simply "gathering together" does not suffice, as it becomes only a temporary relief from the physical phenomenon, in which multiple divided individuals gather in a common shelter. This pragmatic approach to the "why" of church—the need for human companionship—yields a very uncomfortable second point: if, when we gather, the point is "so that we are gathering together," *nothing about our theological situation has been changed in our gathering.*

Additional information may have been absorbed or experiences partaken of, but the practices of our gathering remain calibrated toward seeing gathering (or as Bonhoeffer puts it more pointedly, "hiding") as the end unto itself. And so *how* we gather remains the unexamined element of isolation that remains to be uprooted. To put it succinctly, the opposite of "isolation" is not merely church as "people gathering together"; the opposite of isolation is "community in and through Christ."

Throughout *Life Together*, Bonhoeffer presumes that unless the gathered body is gathered in Christ, it is not Christian community and, by extension, is deficient as a church. Making this sharp claim puts to the side the two faces of isolation (the individual and the crowd) as nonstarters for understanding the nature of church, for to be in Christ is to be in Christ with all others who are in Christ. If the church is the firstfruits of Christ's resurrection, gathered forth from the earth by the Spirit, the emphasis on the church as a bodily communion is inseparable from the church's constitution by the Spirit who attests to the Son. Christ, reigning in heaven, is present through his body in the world; thus, to be a Christian entails bodily presence to the presence of Christ: the gathered people of the church, brought together not as aggregate members but as an interdependent whole. One cannot have Christ's presence apart from the difficulties and banality of other people, any more than one can have the fullness of marriage apart from the difficulties and joys of one's physically present spouse. As Screwtape reminded his understudy demon, the actual physical presence of another person is the crucible in which our theological commitments to "unity" and "love" are forged as something other than ideals.[30]

In many cases, particularly in times of crisis, illness, diminished resources, or distance, it becomes necessary to mediate the distance of persons, and indeed to "gather" the church, by digital means. It is also the fact that many of the activities of church are able to acclimate themselves accordingly: classes may occur over Zoom, meetings over

30. C. S. Lewis, *The Screwtape Letters*, in *The Screwtape Letters and Screwtape Proposes a Toast*, annotated ed. (New York: HarperOne, 2013), 15–16. Screwtape advises the junior demon Wormwood to divert the Christian in the following way: "Keep his mind on the inner life. He thinks his conversion is something *inside* him. . . . You must bring him to a condition in which he can practice self-examination for an hour without discovering any of those facts about himself which are perfectly clear to anyone who has ever lived in the same house with him or worked in the same office."

the phone, even singing as a matter of participating in a livestream. It may be lamentable, but it is possible, to omit physical gathering for various reasons. But is it *wrong* in the way that the description above has been indicating? Does it play into the dynamics I've been describing? Naming something as less than desirable is one thing, but something stronger is at stake here: the ways in which a theological reality is perpetuated in practice.

For any number of practical reasons, such gathering may very well be the only recourse as a matter of expedience or exigency. But this is different than establishing digital mediation as a *substitution* for physical presence, insofar as isolation is a complex phenomenon requiring attention not only to existential dimensions but also to bodily ones. I will allow the proponents of digital mediation to make their own defenses, remaining instead with Bonhoeffer's concern for the ways in which isolation comes to us as a complex phenomenon: bodily, relational, and spiritual.[31] For if this is at the core of the human condition in sin, then any account of digital mediation as equivalent to physical gatherings must account for how it is offering more than simply the practical *representation* of another person to us on the screen. We may certainly represent ourselves in person as much as via digital means, but gathering in bodily presence is less curatable and offers fewer opportunities to distance from one another the fullness of what we are.

31. There are any number of excellent works exploring the possibilities of digital ethics and digital presence, such as Kate Ott, *Christian Ethics for a Digital Society* (Lanham, MD: Rowman & Littlefield, 2018); Angela Williams Gorrell, *Always On: Practicing Faith in a New Media Landscape* (Grand Rapids: Baker Academic, 2019); and the pastoral and moving account of Deanna A. Thompson, *The Virtual Body of Christ in a Suffering World* (Nashville: Abingdon, 2016). My concern is that frequently these forms of digital mediation envision becoming the normative posture for human relations, an evolutionary refinement of human relational capacity, instead of a temporary stopgap. It is true that digital media relations are involved in the "next stage" of human relations, but not in the sense that these digital relations amplify individual agency. By contrast, I would suggest that digital relations further humanity's dependence on a medium that subjects human sociality further to the logic of monetization, furthering the ways in which human flourishing and mediums of mediation monetize those relations, mobilizing our relationality for profit. Our mediation to one another comes at the expense of humanity turned into a product, our relations determined and altered by the primary concern for the profitability of the medium. See Shoshanna Zuboff, *The Age of Surveillance Capitalism: The Fight for a Human Future at the New Frontier of Power* (New York: Public Affairs, 2019).

The challenge that digital forms of mediation must answer, by Bonhoeffer's lights, is this: digital community begins with the scattering of people from one another as the default ground to which our vision of church then must be calibrated. When we construct church in such a way that all of the activities of the church can be fully and completely performed through our own individual thoughts, our own individual agency, our own individual interpretation mediated through our personal digital device, then what we are doing may very well be religiously informative or inspirational, but we will be accommodating to the conditions of isolation, not operating in defiance of them. A community is not destroyed when it cannot physically gather, for there is a rhythm to gathering and scattering, to growing and dying, to rain and sun, to everything under creation. And so there is a season for being alone, which we will discuss. But the separateness of the individual is meant to be *ordered toward* the visible gathering of the community, not assumed as the ideal condition.[32]

While digital representation presents one challenge to the concept of the bodily gathered community, emphasizing the role of the individual in virtual relations, a different challenge arises when bodies *do* gather: the crowd. The crowd, seemingly the opposite of the individual, is rather the group of aggregated individuals. For the crowd allows the individual to retain their individual voice, their individual song, their individual prayer. But the crowd will provide one thing the individual cannot provide themselves: a collective face within which to remain alone or, as Bonhoeffer put it, to hide. In a crowd, no one is at fault for collective actions or held accountable for collective failures of action. Crowds allow individuals to be at home within them and to depart without having anything demanded of them once they are gone. When we have a religious gathering that emphasizes the shared experience, the corporate mission, or the shared song only, we have a crowd: a group of individuals who are *incidentally* in the same place, having the same experience, but

32. It is here that Bonhoeffer calls this union one of "vicarious representative action," a loving of others that puts us representatively in their place as we act on their behalf and for their good. For the ethical contours of this, and why it matters for community life, see Christine Schliesser, *Everyone Who Acts Responsibly Becomes Guilty: Bonhoeffer's Concept of Accepting Guilt* (Louisville: Westminster John Knox, 2008).

who remain effectively alone, having nothing required of them other than their performance and with no connection established with any other participants.

There is a sense in which the crowd is the precursor to the community, in that the crowd offers articulations of value that the individual may have been too timid to speak alone. As Willie James Jennings puts it, "The crowd was not his disciples, but it was the condition for discipleship. It is the ground to which all discipleship will return, always aiming at the crowd that is the gathering of hurting and hungry people who need God. . . . Like a mother offering her body to her hungry child, so the crowd is necessary to see God's overwhelming compassion."[33] Jennings is right here to argue that, whatever we say about the community, it must not forget from whence it came, and it must not abandon that world which frequently surprises us and will not submit to techniques of order. We will return to this in detail later, but for now I will offer only this: while the crowd is, in one way or another, a corporate articulation of desire (for healing, for relief, in anger), these articulations must be channeled into a different form—that of the community.

The first way in which the community differs from these alternatives of the crowd and the individual is that in a community, one's will is never absolute but finds its object (and limit) in another person. By contrast, Bonhoeffer notes, when I am alone, my will for myself becomes absolute, and when I am in a crowd, I will only alongside others. But in a community, my will finds a limit in the desires, the thoughts, the needs, and the body of another.[34] The community begins to mirror what we saw in the original vision of Genesis, of persons contingent on one another. As we come to be able to articulate the ways in which our wills align and join with one another, we form a community—a body of persons whose wills come together, recognizing that their willing toward one another, and not against

33. Jennings, *After Whiteness*, 13.
34. Bonhoeffer, *Sanctorum Communio*, 73. This element of the will finding its limit in the person of another is significant, for the person is composed of bodiliness, not just an image of the person or an idea of the person when they encounter another. As we saw already in his treatment of the garden, the will that engages other bodies finds a real (and gracious) limit in other people: to desire otherwise is to desire to dominate a person treated as an idea.

one another, is how they now live.[35] The crowd dissipates when their common reason for joining has ended, but the community—because it exists through us not just willing a common purpose but willing *one another together*—endures, though the material reasons for our gathering might change.

The community, then, is a living exchange, something that grows and changes as its members grow and change. Their life together, though spoken about in certain objective ways ("We do these things," and "This is what it's like when we're together"), is generated by those who are a part of the community.[36] When the city of Abilene (where I live) deliberates, celebrates, and works for the good of neighbors together—when we commit to each other regardless of what civic project is at hand, not simply during election seasons or disasters—it does so as a civic community, operating as a whole. But apart from these moments, groups—Abilene included—function mostly as crowds, even if their members are structurally knit together by civic codes, taxes, and common laws or if their members join together in tactical allegiances.

The *church*-community differs here from the more general definition further, in that in the church, the Spirit of God moves through the relations of the community, binding members together, purifying their wills, bringing the virtues of Christ into their deliberations of purpose and the fruits of the Spirit into their celebrations and into the common labors for neighbor. In the church, Bonhoeffer writes, the self becomes porous, open to others, though not dissolved;[37] we become not a crowd of indistinguishable faces but a people joined together into a differentiated body, with divided wills brought into union by Christ, who joins us together.[38] The community, through willing the good of others, begins the movement away from being a crowd, but it is through being united by Christ's mediation of one person to another that the *church*-community appears.

The church-community, like a crowd, is certainly composed of whatever individuals come to it: one does not have to enter into

35. Bonhoeffer, *Sanctorum Communio*, 84.
36. Bonhoeffer, *Sanctorum Communio*, 99.
37. Bonhoeffer, *Sanctorum Communio*, 117.
38. Bonhoeffer, *Sanctorum Communio*, 136.

the church as part of a preexisting relationship, be it as a parent, child, spouse, or friend. And, like crowds, when you depart from the church-community, you will depart back into the same home and the same network of relationships whence you came. But two aspects differ here.

First, because a community is constituted through the joining of wills together, the church-community does not view the individual as the telos of the gathering, in the way that individualism and crowds do: the church-community incorporates (without negating or eclipsing) the person and in doing so calls out the gifts, experiences, agency, and abilities of all members. Second, and as importantly, the church-community, because it is that which involves the will directed toward others, *requires* something of the individual. It makes demands, places obligations, and requires participation, such that the individual and the community will be altered not only in their time gathered but *as they depart*. They will be changed, not because they have had some affective encounter but because their understanding of self, the purpose of their gifts, their self-determination of knowledge, and the like are not left without challenge by the others gathered. It is only when the individual is viewed as *inviolable*—"buffered," to use Charles Taylor's language—in these respects that the language of "community" really means simply a dressed-up version of the phenomenon of the crowd.

The church is meant to be a community, and not eclipsed by individualism or by the crowd, for in the church-community, we share in Christ and each other and are changed by that exchange. There is no escaping being "in Adam," for the church is a body where the world "in Adam"—with all of its creaturely contours, bonds, and fractures—is taken up and transfigured into the body of Christ. But when we find ourselves unable to gather, two things will be indicators that our thinking and practice are already in the grips of isolation. First, much of what we do is able to be packaged for the individual, for it is already designed in this way: nothing is lost for lack of the presence of others. And second, when we gather again, it will be as a crowd, a gathering in which response is neither required nor expected and where no opening to the outside, including to the persons next to us, is needed—either in word, deed, or presence. We will enter and leave undisturbed by the presence of others, and even by the words spoken, for they too remain as utterances that make no immediate claim on us, as information to be taken up or put down. Ultimately, if what the church is can be performed by the individual without remainder, then we gather not because anything is materially altered in us when we gather but because we wish to not be doing these alone.

Christian Community: The Renewal of Creation and of the Knowledge of God

To see this difference that "community" makes for how we know God—over against the claims of the individual and the crowd—we need to detour briefly into Bonhoeffer's roots, into his less well-known but important dissertations published as *Sanctorum Communio* and *Act and Being*.[39] Describing the church involves two inextricable claims: (1) Christianity cannot *not* be social—that is, there is no such thing as a nonsocial life in Christ. And (2) Christianity is not *merely* social—that is, the church is not only a social institution but a gathered body within creation that is the body of the risen Son of God. There is no disentangled origin to being social and being in Christ, for the two come into view together.[40]

The implication of this major claim—that our life in Christ and our lives with others are intertwined—affects a number of theological claims and topics. As is commonly claimed, a doctrine of sin (though not adopted by Bonhoeffer in this way) operates in this socially knit kind of way: there is no space in which I might be absolutely free of sin, as we exist in a common creation afflicted by sin, and as such, I remain obligated not only to my own sin but responsible to the effects that sin has on others as well. Bonhoeffer's counterclaim to sin with respect to the church, then, affects how we think of our redemption in Christ—that there is no sense in which *my* salvation is disentangled from the salvation of all those who are in Christ.[41]

39. Dietrich Bonhoeffer, *Act and Being: Transcendental Philosophy and Ontology in Systematic Theology*, trans. H. Martin Rumscheidt, Dietrich Bonhoeffer Works 2 (Minneapolis: Fortress, 1996).

40. Bonhoeffer, *Sanctorum Communio*, 63.

41. Consider Hebrews 11:39–40 in this fashion, where the author writes, "Yet all these, though they were commended for their faith, did not receive what was

To desire a salvation that is not social is, in other words, to desire a world other than the one created by God: one in which I can exist in isolation from others.

The presumption of anthropology—that we are "persons"—occurs in this matrix of social life, not prior to it. Whether considered with respect to the development of language or our naming of ourselves as an "I," the social precedes our sense of individual agency: our selves always come mediated to us by the relations we have with others.[42] As we have seen, it is in community that our wills find their limits, conveying the truth that what we are is, by God's grace, not without bounds and not self-determined. Without such a body to belong to—one in which our wills are coordinated together toward some end, mediated together—we are left with only the possibility of the literal war of all against all. Apart from a community, in the conflicted and agonistic war of all, not only does each person forget the debts toward that which made them but we forget that it is a community that makes the self we wrongly claim as ours alone possible in the first place.[43]

But—even if this framework of community is sociologically plausible—what does this have to do with *God*? Here, Bonhoeffer puts two competing accounts of revelation into conversation, to construct an account of how humans receive the revelation of God within time and what implications this has for the church. The first version— "act" ontology—describes God's revelation as interruptive, creating a dialectical difference between God and creation, between God's eternity and created time, between the singularity of divine speech and the multitude of human language. In this model, we encounter God as the one who creates a crisis of the self within the flow of time and within their own history. Here, God creates people as singular hearers, broken away from their other commitments in the world; the hearer of God's revelation is placed into the truth, in an atemporal

---

promised, since God had provided something better so that they would not, apart from us, be made perfect." One could read this as a simple covenantal claim: the saints before Christ are not complete apart from the saints after Christ. Or, as we have been arguing, one could read this as making the canonical claim in addition to the social claim: that salvation is a corporate affair and not one that will be accomplished by the claiming of aggregated souls.

42. Bonhoeffer, *Sanctorum Communio*, 69, 73.
43. Bonhoeffer, *Sanctorum Communio*, 84–88.

fashion where time and context have little meaning and therefore all history and culture are judged and found wanting by God.[44]

When one reads the Scripture, it is easy (as evidenced by the work of the early Karl Barth and that of Søren Kierkegaard) to find examples that seem to indicate that God speaks as a lightning bolt that rends the heavens and stops the clock: Abraham, Saul en route to Damascus, Moses at the burning bush. The issue for Bonhoeffer here with this being a full picture of how God speaks is not that God displaces all other relationships and relativizes the absoluteness of history, including Israel's history. The issue here is that, if this is the total picture of how God reveals who God is, there can be no continuity of any kind in creation: it would mean that God's word, as purely eternal, has no point of contact within the flow of history. We would live only from moment to moment listening for God's voice, with no way to live as creatures of time and history, and certainly no sense of having a past that would be anything other than a threat to God's speech. In its extreme, it would mean that human community is what *prevents* people from hearing the voice of God. "Church," in this extreme reading, is thus not a body of persons joined to one another but only a body of co-*hearers*, individuals each standing *coram Deo* but not needing one another in any substantial way.

As we have been discussing it, this way of understanding revelation makes isolation a *necessary* principle of church gathering: if we can rightly hear God only when we are singular, we cannot be committed to one another over time in any way—whether parent to child, husband to wife, or friend to stranger—without compromising the absolute nature of the way God reveals God's self. This necessary division *between* persons also introduces a division *within* the person. I cannot have any sense of continuity of my own selfhood over time; the relationship between what I am now, as one who hears God, and what I will be or have been cannot ever be assumed: the "I" who hears God exists only now, in this moment. I become cut off from the support of others; the knowledge of what God is and what God desires rests solely on my shoulders, and I have no other resources I can turn to without compromising the nature of revelation.

44. Bonhoeffer, *Act and Being*, 90–92.

The solution here, however, is not to reject *any* sense of personal agency and to lose any sense of individuated identity or personal hearing from God, retreating into a crowd. The second version of revelation that Bonhoeffer considers—revelation as an extended historical event in which I situate myself—has its own deficiencies. To describe revelation as that which is found within a specific history—as a kind of *being* that I join—is to commit the opposite error to the first account. In this second account, God is locked into a historical flow, making God *only* a historical force and not the God who exists separate from creation. As opposed to God interrupting creation here and there, God is enmeshed in and dependent on a specific history, without which God cannot be known or encountered. In this second version, then, the revelation of God is given to a historical institution invested with absolute historical meaning, an institution that performs the same judgments of God's revelation as the isolated individual did, only at an institutional level.[45] The value of the person that the former version (act) absolutizes is lost entirely if one has only the latter (being).

While it is right and good to say that we encounter God in history, Christians have long noted that God comes to us through creation but not *as* creation, that there is a distinction between God and creation that persists even in God's presence to us, such that institutional claims to the knowledge of God can be made only contingently, known as we go and not as finalized judgments. The intimacy of God to creation persists as a cloud out in front of the people and as Jesus, whom the disciples both knew and did not fully understand. Likewise, we are the people of God not by grasping and concretizing the mystery of God as a blueprint for our action, reducing God to that which is possessed either by the individual as the intuition of conscience or by the crowd as an objectified history. Rather, we know God by being led in prayer and trust into a future we cannot name by a God whom we know but cannot capture.

It is in this that the church as a community offers something very different: a community that receives the gift of God's presence from the outside in the very act of being joined together by God over time,

45. Bonhoeffer, *Act and Being*, 103–5.

doing so together within the ongoing flux and frailty of history. It is only in this way—by journeying together in time—that we receive God: "Christian revelation must occur in the present precisely because it is, in the qualified once-and-for-all occurrence of the cross and resurrection of Christ, always something 'of the future.' It must, in other words, be thought in the church, for the church is the present Christ, 'Christ existing as community.'"[46]

The other options of God's revelation—the isolated individual or the historical crowd—both describe how we receive God, but do so either, for example, by surrendering Peter qua Peter to being a part of the crowd or by cutting Peter off from the other disciples. In order to bring these two together—the attention to the person and to social bodies—a third element is added: time. Christ's presence to the gathered body is one that Bonhoeffer narrates carefully in terms of the church as a *way*, not the endpoint: the church is the body that does not capture God in its historical existence but learns over time of the God who comes to us, creatures of time, from beyond creation.[47]

Because we are creatures bound up and given existence together in time, we do not encounter God as a singular individual apart from others, nor do we give up our selfhood and encounter God as just another feature of history, captured by the ebbs and flows of time. We encounter God knit together as God's people, *in and through* time, led through time with others on the basis of God's promises: God will always lead us, and God will remain present to us—we live in hope, trusting that our lives together, which are given to us in creation, are not an obstacle to God's presence but part of the way in which we know God.

God's revelation occurs, then, within history as a way, making *discipleship*—the art of living the Christian life in the world—not a secondary feature but an intrinsic dimension of being church and of knowing God.[48] The Holy Spirit draws together a body, which

46. Bonhoeffer, *Act and Being*, 111.

47. This tension is summed up well by Derek Taylor when he writes that for Bonhoeffer, "the community exists because Christ is present; Christ is never present simply because a community exists." Derek W. Taylor, *Reading Scripture as the Church: Dietrich Bonhoeffer's Hermeneutic of Discipleship* (Downers Grove, IL: IVP Academic, 2020), 40.

48. On this, see Andre Dumas, *Dietrich Bonhoeffer: Theologian of Reality* (London: SCM, 1971), 168.

then proceeds, in the presence of the Lord, across time, following the lead of the Lord, who goes out in front of it.[49] We do not, as it were, receive the revelation of God and then "do something" with that revelation—this would be the model of the isolated hearer, who somehow encounters God apart from their entanglement with history or other disciples. Discipleship, rather, is an apprenticeship to the living Christ, revealed to the church in the reading of the Scriptures, in the celebration of the bread and the cup, and in the processes of *being the church*: we learn Christ as we learn to be Christ's disciples, encountering God only as we receive God together over time.

In terms of the isolation of sin, this account is significant for two reasons. First, the way out of the isolation that sin names is not simply a matter of the individual being reconciled to God; for all of the attractiveness of this "act"-based form of revelation, this way of thinking about revelation continues to fragment the individual from both time and creation as well as from all other hearers. Likewise, God's revelation is not a kind of purely commodifiable object addressed to hearers who are able to make absolute judgments over the veracity of the word spoken to them, as though we were in a crowd; God addresses persons who were meant to be knit together by Christ, over time. To be a redeemed creature of God is to be restored to the fullness of God's redemption: remade into a community before God, by God, as we follow God together.

But second, this community that is being redeemed by the work of Christ is interconnected with the world it shares with the rest of God's creation: it does not assume an ahistorical posture but is interwoven with creation, such that there can be no retreat or withdrawal from creation ultimately. As we saw, the church is drawn into Christ, but it never fully leaves behind the marks of being "in Adam." The renewal of community that the church undergoes is that which it is able to extend into the world as well through its natural bonds of

49. Bonhoeffer is repeatedly accused of Christomonism in his theology, of collapsing all categories into his Christology, but this is simply an uncareful reading. Repeatedly—most notably in *Life Together* but also across his writings and lectures to his students—Bonhoeffer assumes the work of the Holy Spirit to be the work of the triune God, who unites believers to the work of Christ, though this is a union that occurs as the disciples enter into the work of witness into the world.

time, history, and vocation. As Bonhoeffer will put it most cogently in *Ethics*, "When one therefore wants to speak of the space of the church, one must be aware that this space has already been broken through, abolished, and overcome in every moment by the witness of the church to Jesus Christ. Thus all false thinking in terms of realms is ruled out as endangering the understanding of the church."[50]

The church that hears God together is conceived of as a dynamic body over time, proceeding as Christ's body across time by the work of the Spirit. The church is perpetually on the way, but not out of a need to be progressive, constantly revising who it thinks God is; the God of Abraham, Isaac, and Jacob is the God of today, and so Christians learn what it means to follow God today by listening to the words of Scripture and the wisdom of the church while not being bound to *being* Abraham, Isaac, or Jacob.

As we are joined to the community of the church, we lose our isolation (in ceasing to be divided from God and from others) and become the *persons* (the interconnected creatures of God) we were meant to be: members of Christ's body and members of one another. We are rejoined to God and to others as we follow Christ together. The church follows its Lord in history, working out its salvation in fear and trembling, calling the world to Christ as it proceeds into the world. And as it does so, the various dimensions of isolation—between persons (as we are knit together into one community), between God and humanity (as we unlearn the fragmenting ways of sin), and between the church and creation (as we call the world out of its fragmentation)—are undone.[51]

The Church in the World, the Church for the World

By now we have been able to see why community—a body of persons woven together over time as they journey together with Christ—is of

---

50. Dietrich Bonhoeffer, *Ethics*, trans. Reinhard Krauss, Charles C. West, and Douglass W. Stott, Dietrich Bonhoeffer Works 6 (Minneapolis: Fortress, 2005), 64. On this theme, see Ulrik Becker Nissen, "Letting Reality Become Real: On Mystery and Reality in Dietrich Bonhoeffer's Ethics," *Journal of Religious Ethics* 39 (2011): 321–43.

51. For a detailed account of Bonhoeffer's first dissertation, *Sanctorum Communio*, see Michael Mawson, *Christ Existing as Community: Bonhoeffer's Ecclesiology* (Oxford: Oxford University Press, 2018).

such deep significance not only for how God undoes the sin embedded within our lives but for what it means that the church knows Christ. As we have been discussing, isolation is the marker of sin in the world, and it is the work of God in Christ to restore communion between creation and God. To be the church, then, means not only to participate in the work that Christ is working out through this body of people but that the union that Christ brings here will be the property of all creation: God will redeem the creation that this people shares with their neighbors.

In the prologue of John, we find that all things in creation—even those that reject Christ—are upheld by Christ. Christ comes to those who are his own—those created in and through Christ—such that their rejection does not occur in any other world than one upheld by Christ. And so the church—led through the world in faithfulness, being healed from its isolation as it is led forward—is not all of what God is concerned with. As Herbert McCabe puts it, in John's Gospel, Christ's presence in creation, both in his person and his way, is sacramental, leading what God has made back home.[52]

By virtue of their constitution as creatures of God, all persons inside and outside the church are, in a very real sense then, already included in the work of Christ, for all persons exist through no other reason than that they are created by the Word. The church, as the image of Christ in the world, renders in its living what all creation is to be like. And so we can say without crossing our fingers that the Christ of the church is the center of all creation, in this way: both church and world exist *only* in and through the Word, with the church displaying this truth in its proclamation and its life when it invites the world to follow the Christ it proclaims. In Christ we see the curse of Adam undone, but undone *collectively*: "It is 'Adam,' a collective person, who can only be superseded by the collective person 'Christ existing as church-community.' . . . The humanity of sin is one, *though consisting of nothing but individuals. It is a collective person, yet infinitely fragmented. . . . This duality is its essence, and it is superseded . . . only through the unity of the new humanity in Christ.*"[53]

52. Herbert McCabe, *God Matters* (London: Continuum, 2005), 48–51.
53. Bonhoeffer, *Sanctorum Communio*, 121 (emphasis original).

Humans were created to be in visible community, a community that "in Adam" exists only as a crowd but that in Christ exists as the church, as Adam is raised up and made into Christ's body. We move from one to the other by the power of the Spirit, not by abandoning creation, for Christ's call approaches us through the folds of creation.[54]

Christ calls his church into being not by abolishing the contingencies of creation that shape the church but by drawing out the poison from creation in its veins: turning tax collectors into generous benefactors, religious zealots into merciful teachers of the law, prostitutes into exemplars of chastity. We move from Adam to Christ as God renews us *in* creation, with the world around the church renewed as an extension of this. The life together of the church, then, is intrinsic to what it means for God to remake the world because the church is connected to the creation God wants to remake in all kinds of ways, for Adam is caught up in Christ: the church is embedded and inextricably bound to the dying Adam whom God wills to bring to life.

There is no particular language Christians speak, though Christians use particular words like *God* and *justice* in ways different from how others use them. There is no particular way that Christians use their mouths to eat, though what Christians eat, whom they eat with, and the limits to our consumption are all changed by Christ. All kinds of people parent and care for their families, though what it means to be a Christian disciple and parent is subject to a host of different concerns and considerations. All of these activities shared by Christians and others are pathways and connections to the community, the community centered in Christ that transfigures the whole of creation.

All of this is to say that there is no false divide between the "mission" of the church and the "being" of the church: the way the church images the work of Christ is by being the church both in its scattering and in its gathering. Sin submerges creation in isolation in both subtle and overt ways, and often the church perpetuates this power of death without realizing it, a tendency—because of sharing the common world of Adam—that the church will never be free from. But this is not an occasion for despair, but trust: that even our

54. I am indebted to Christopher W. Moore for this phrase.

repetitions of the fall will be taken up by God and renewed and that these links between church and creation will be those God uses to "take up space" in the world.[55]

Finding Our Way Home

In this chapter, we have unpacked Bonhoeffer's concern for the ways in which creation is fragmented by sin, making isolation our default assumption as well as how the church-community is intrinsic to what salvation is. Christ gathers us up into a community, into a renewed vision of what all creation is meant to be. Our life together as the church is thus an extended life of discipleship, of the healing of the wounds of sin as we journey together with God. If it is in being joined to the community of Christ that we not only come to know the revelation of Christ but also are healed from the isolation so pervasive in our human condition, the practices and insights of the church are not simply strategies for "cultivating community," for church growth, or for missions, as important as these goals are. They are for the healing of the body of Christ from this primal wound, this isolation that is the mark of sin, so that we might participate in Christ's own work: to heal a creation broken and isolated by the fall.

To be able to more clearly view the possibilities that come here, however, we must first come to terms with how isolation takes root in the church. So we will ask two questions:

In what ways does the gathered church perpetuate isolation?
What difference does the church-community make then?

---

55. Dietrich Bonhoeffer, *Discipleship*, trans. Barbara Green and Reinhard Krauss, Dietrich Bonhoeffer Works 4 (Minneapolis: Fortress, 2001), 225. On this image, see Donald Fergus, "Lebensraum—Just What Is This 'Habitat' or 'Living Space' That Dietrich Bonhoeffer Claimed for the Church?," *Scottish Journal of Theology* 67 (2014): 70–84. In direct mimicking of the language used by the Nazis as a kind of territorial expansion, Bonhoeffer uses this phrase to describe the infiltration of the church into all the world, spatialized, but without territory.

Two

The Church and the Practice of Isolation

Isolation seeps into the practices of the church in so many ways that we could never name them all, any more than one can name the multitudes of sin's novelties. But taxonomies, such as the one employed in this chapter, are helpful, not because they name every possible species but because they give us lenses that enable us to see new species when they appear.

Before we can begin seeing the way out of the isolation of sin, we must first come to terms with those supporting elements of our church life that are themselves perpetuating isolation, and how they do this. Whenever Christ gathers the body, it gathers under a variety of cultural signs, languages, and degrees of material support and with no small latitude of local customs: the church is not an idea but a theological reality, born in the world by the Spirit's ingathering of Christ's people. And so the temptation to isolation takes these myriad material forms as well.

With this taxonomy, we will explore these two ways in which isolation is perpetuated by church practice: by making Christians into individuals and by making them into crowds. In offering these criticisms, I do not imply that we should discard practices of singing, of reading, of discipleship, of eating, or of leadership; rather, I present a way for us to see that *how* we gather remains as important as what we do when we gather. For practices without ends in mind will have an end provided for them: further isolation and division.

The Drive to Survive

In an increasingly post-Christian world, the drive for survival offers powerful temptations to sustain in the short term even practices that are killing us in the long term: making church accessible to individuals or accommodated to crowds. And for a good many years, these practices may have worked. In Bonhoeffer's own day, the existing network for training German ministers was expansive and well moneyed and drew from the embarrassment of riches in the university system.[1] Ministers were paid through the state, pensioned into retirement, and without many material worries. That Bonhoeffer himself finished his doctoral work before the age of twenty-five was not entirely unusual, in that advanced education for ministers was expected. The result was a wealth of preaching, scholarship, connection, and cohesiveness for the German Lutheran churches.

I mention Bonhoeffer's own situation at the outset to highlight the analogy between his era and the present with respect to stability and the dangers of calibrating the success of the church to metrics of stable numbers or influence. Much work has been done on the decline of participation in American churches, a trend that will likely continue in the years to come.[2] Although church attendance remains a cultural

1. The relationship between the German ministerial training system and the German educational system in Bonhoeffer's day was entangled with imperial aspirations and with viewing religion as integral to cultural development. The implications for viewing church as part of a social crowd will become clear. For an overview, see Detlef Müller, Fritz Ringer, and Brian Simons, eds., *The Rise of the Modern Educational System: Structural Change and Social Reproduction, 1870–1920* (Cambridge: Cambridge University Press, 1989); and H. George Anderson, "Challenge and Change within German Protestant Theological Education during the Nineteenth Century," *Church History* 39 (1970): 36–48. For more focused discussion of German theological education during Bonhoeffer's era, see Thomas Albert Howard, *Protestant Theology and the Making of the Modern German University* (Oxford: Oxford University Press, 2006), 267–402.

2. For the sociological data on this trend, see Robert P. Jones, *The End of White Christian America* (New York: Simon & Schuster, 2017); Ronald F. Inglehart, *Religion's Sudden Decline: What's Causing It and What Comes Next?* (Oxford: Oxford

possibility even in the most secularized portions of the country, and is at times assumed because of the church's long-standing cultural presence, signs of weakening abound. Similar presumptions exist, both in Bonhoeffer's situation and ours, that in some meaningful way the present draw for church will continue on indefinitely—that funding will exist and that people will always want to come to church. But the danger is that we become used to thinking of this historical contingency as *necessary* and of an abundance of resources as *essential*, such that when one of those things changes, we pragmatically shift gears to sustain past norms of attendance or participation, not realizing that we may be using pattens of operation that are themselves part of the problem.

Put sharply, the shift in cultural supports and the drop of attendance patterns (combined with anxiety about equating attendance patterns with divine sanction) reveals an important truth: the gathering of the church is a gift and thus sustained only by God's calling by the Spirit, not by the ebb and flow of cultural support. What has made the church thrive and exist was never that it was clever or well moneyed or that it had a right to gather, and what designated its faithfulness was not that it was well attended. These things aided and assisted, but frequently the things that assist the church's gathering work at odds with the church's nature; in Bonhoeffer's own day, the German Evangelical Church—which pledged its allegiance to the Führer as the head of the church—survived as a social institution but at the cost of amplifying the sin and isolation it was called to be an alternative to, amplifying German nationalism and denigrating God's people, the Jews.[3] The German Evangelical Church survived, but only by being a crowd, unified by its cultural trappings or social connections, instead of rejecting the isolation created by sin and being a unified body of Christ capable of sustaining Jew and gentile in one body.

University Press, 2021); and Paul Silas Peterson, ed., *The Decline of Established Christianity in the Western World: Interpretations and Responses* (New York: Routledge, 2017). Interpretations of this phenomenon vary, and global expressions of Christianity remain steady and growing, but what remains common in these analyses is the link between the loss of cultural supports and the decline of participation in church attendance or congregational involvement.

3. Wolfgang Gerlach, *And the Witnesses Were Silent: The Confessing Church and the Persecution of the Jews* (Lincoln: University of Nebraska Press, 2000).

A church can attempt to bypass this kind of contingency in innumerable ways by becoming a kind of "durable" church capable of weathering cultural declines.[4] By adopting either the "individual" or "crowd" model borrowed from the world around it, churches may attempt to overcome decline. In the former, we weather the loss of cultural support for church by turning the church into a content creator, supplying believers with information for their consumption. In the latter, we weather the shifting winds by gathering in as many as we can by any means necessary, creating experiences for a crowd and shying away from whatever might scatter them.

The former temptation, however, ultimately forces the individual to be the arbiter of truth and of God's own presence, and it fails for precisely this reason: the individual, making judgments about God's presence or absence and God's nature, essence, or will, does so by making God subject to the forms of reasoning we take as normative; God can never be anything but a kind of knowledge we already anticipate and which we judge in its truth or falsehood. Gone is a God who would actually appear under the surprising sign of the burning bush or the God who would rise from the dead, replaced by a god who aligns with some capacity we already are familiar with.[5] The latter temptation—the cultivation of the crowd—fails because it assumes

4. I draw this distinction from Nassim Nicholas Taleb's *Antifragile: Things That Gain from Disorder* (New York: Random House, 2014), in which he proposes that "durable" institutions are those that survive disorder through duplication and redundancy, operating according to core principles of the past, hardening their categories and modalities, whereas "antifragile" institutions are those that thrive on improvisation and learn from the mistakes of the past. In this analogy, the church that seeks the durability it needs to weather cultural change only duplicates the isolationist tendencies of the surrounding world rather than embracing the opportunity that comes with cultural loss. I am indebted to Matthew Shedden for drawing my attention to this work.

5. In an interesting twist, Bonhoeffer finds that Karl Barth winds up being guilty of this tendency: describing God in "act" terms—asserting that we know God only when God acts—entails that the question of judging *when* and *how* God is acting inevitably is mediated by personal faculties of reason or judgment (Dietrich Bonhoeffer, *Act and Being: Transcendental Philosophy and Ontology in Systematic Theology*, trans. H. Martin Rumscheidt, Dietrich Bonhoeffer Works 2 [Minneapolis: Fortress, 1996], 87–91). As Clark Elliston rightly points out, Bonhoeffer is endlessly worried about the ways in which "conscience" is, in practice, simply a mirror for what we were going to do anyway (*Dietrich Bonhoeffer and the Ethical Self: Christology, Ethics, and Formation* [Minneapolis: Fortress, 2016], 47).

that gathering becomes the end unto itself, even if gatherings do not overcome or address the separation that exists between persons. The church-as-crowd, having emphasized gathering as the end unto itself, will become replaced by some greater or more accomplished crowd, even if the next crowd has little do with Christ crucified and resurrected.

When we come to terms with the difficulties of survival—recognizing, indeed, that even churches, as organisms in the world, die—then it becomes easier for us to let go of those ways of operating even when they are still currently working. Michael Jinkins, in *The Church Faces Death*, rightly suggests that "the assumption behind this anxiety and the supposition that undergirds a large proportion of the literature is that if the church simply remained faithful . . . it would not decline."[6] Those committed to the proposals above would indeed name their work as faithfulness, a willingness to stretch out, to try new things, to boldly embrace new trends, to be "all things to all people" (1 Cor. 9:22), and I do not contest their intent. But the concern Jinkins names here (which I share) is this: that in trying to escape the crumbling conditions of death, we abandon what grounds the church, the enduring presence of Christ to the gathered church, trading it for modes of operation that endear it to the world "in Adam."[7]

Jinkins lays a difficult truth before churches: it is very possible that churches will die, and calibrating the church to the isolation of the world will not save them. But this only points us to the ways in which church is a gift, a body to be lived into, and not a constructed form that staves off decline. In this world, the gathering of the church-community in bodily form is, in truth, a true privilege, and the church has been given signs by which to recognize this.[8] When gathering

6. Michael Jinkins, *The Church Faces Death* (Oxford: Oxford University Press, 1999), 13.

7. Jinkins, *Church Faces Death*, 98: "Catholicity is grounded in particularity, and if one abandons the immediate one will miss the eternal altogether. By confessing first our provincial perspectives, we are free to hear the provincial witnesses of one another, and our contradictions can save us from idolatrous claims on behalf of the truth to which we lay claim." Put differently, it is in the particularity of how God gathers the church in its ordinary circumstances that God meets us, not in trying to abandon that place and fleeing our creaturely conditions of demise.

8. Dietrich Bonhoeffer, *Life Together*, trans. Daniel W. Bloesch, in *Life Together; Prayerbook of the Bible*, Dietrich Bonhoeffer Works 5 (Minneapolis: Fortress, 1996), 27–28.

ceases—whether by increased secularization, by forced separation, or by pandemic—the church must take its cues from those who have suffered this isolation all along (the imprisoned, the sick, the scattered lonely, the proclaimers of the gospel in far-flung lands) in order to see this gratuity of gathering.[9] These who bear isolation all the time are not meant to be objects of our pity but to give us vision as to what is essential to our gathering: "The prisoner, the sick person, the Christian living in the diaspora recognizes in the nearness of a fellow Christian a physical sign of the gracious presence of the triune God. They receive each other's blessings as the blessing of the Lord Jesus Christ."[10]

In this description of the meeting of the isolated Christian with their visitor, a real asymmetry of power is present: the prisoner meeting with the free, the quarantined with the well, the exile with the compatriot. But it is precisely *this asymmetry of social standing* that demonstrates that they know that what joins them together is nothing other than the free gift of God, not the result of clever marketing or cultural supports or even common social standing within the surrounding community. In Revelation, the churches that are gathered are nearly all frail and failing, with their goodness existing mostly in tatters and at the edges of John's descriptions of them. They are the seven candlesticks not because they are the best funded or the most socially well positioned but because they are the bodies of Christ scattered into the world. And John would be privileged to be among even the most fragile of them.

It is signs like these—the perpetually isolated who find community, the frail church who lives the gospel—that disabuse us of the illusion that our union with God and others is a matter of institutional belonging, cultural support, or the common time of life that members of a church share.[11] The life of the church-community is a gift to be

9. Bonhoeffer, *Life Together*, 18.

10. Bonhoeffer, *Life Together*, 29. On this theme of the exemplary role of the marginalized in Bonhoeffer, see Lisa Dahill, *Reading from the Underside of Selfhood: Bonhoeffer and Spiritual Formation* (Eugene, OR: Wipf & Stock, 2009).

11. It is for this reason, among others, that Bonhoeffer found the practice of youth ministry, which cordoned off the youth to their own separate space apart from the church, to be abominable. By extension, the presumption that church ministry must be ordered around common life experiences, "life stages," age, or interest should

received, and through it, Christ knits back together the fragments of the world. But before we can turn to recovering what this vision might entail in practice, we must attend to the ways in which our church practice has perpetuated isolation, the ways in which we stave off dissolution and the death of our churches through, ironically, practices built on the premise of isolation.

Isolation and Church Gathering: The Temptation of the Individual

It is a strange claim, if isolation is one of the marks of the fall, that churches have been participating in the *perpetuation* of isolation rather than mitigating it. But in sin, all persons are caught up in Adam and exist together as fractured and isolated individuals; in Christ, all creation is caught up toward redemption, with the church as the firstfruits of that redemption.[12] To be gathered up as the church is to mirror for creation what it was meant for, but not to be in a state separated from creation. This is not to say, however, that every gathering of people embodies this redemptive work of Christ. Even if one acknowledges that bodily gathering is necessary and even fitting for the communion we have with one another as humans and sets aside the error of Christianity-as-individualism, there are innumerable ways of gathering but remaining in hiding, creating a crowd that furthers our division from one another and from God.

In making this approach, let us be clear that the individual in their particularity is not lost or forgotten, though in a qualified fashion: "Jesus' call to discipleship makes the disciple into a single individual. Whether disciples want to or not, they have to make a decision; each has to decide alone. It is not their choice to desire to be single individuals. Individuals suddenly discover all their responsibilities and

---

be called into question as simply contributing to the church's isolating patterns. For Bonhoeffer's critique of youth ministry—and by extension, other "like-minded" ministry groupings—see Andrew Root, *Bonhoeffer as Youth Worker* (Grand Rapids: Baker Academic, 2014).

12. The church is not immune from the effects of the fall but rather brokers the redemption of Christ from within that prior common condition it shares with all creation. See Michael Mawson, *Christ Existing as Community: Bonhoeffer's Ecclesiology* (Oxford: Oxford University Press, 2018), 101–18, for the best explication of this dynamic.

cling to them."[13] Such a strong statement, offered here in *Discipleship*, seems utterly at odds with what we've seen so far. Bonhoeffer, after so strongly emphasizing the Christian community as intrinsic to the way we are healed, suddenly seems to call for a kind of Christianity that is all about the individual: *Reject the group! Let your individuality shine free!* But as we read further, we find that this breaking apart is only a *precursory* movement so that a person may be freed from their false attachments in order to be reintegrated into a *new* body: Christ's own body.

The reign of the individual in church is, at times, more obvious to us, particularly in the form of digital connection. As Angela Williams Gorrell argues, new media outlets offer the opportunity for encountering new stories of discipleship that would otherwise not be locally available and for seeing new vistas for participating in the journey of discipleship.[14] The individual at their screen is opened to a world beyond her own mind and has her thinking enriched. But individuals do this at a cost: these media platforms do not exist in a neutral form but are monetized and ordered toward making us— the user—into a commodity. Our self-disclosure on these platforms encourages facilitating connection not around mundane and ordinary aspects of our lives but around the exemplary and individuating aspects of a person: we do not post about our breakfast or the morning walk, but about our highlights, our exceptional thoughts, our most piquant emotions. These are the grist of the digital landscape, the way in which digital media help us, in the end, not to join others but to curate ourselves.[15] The ironic outcome of this, as Sherry Turkle argues, is that we begin to expect more not out of the people we encounter through digital life but out of the *digital life*, expecting less and less out of the ones we encounter through the screen and more from the technology.[16]

13. Dietrich Bonhoeffer, *Discipleship*, trans. Barbara Green and Reinhard Krauss, Dietrich Bonhoeffer Works 4 (Minneapolis: Fortress, 2001), 92.
14. Angela Williams Gorrell, *Always On: Practicing Faith in a New Media Landscape* (Grand Rapids: Baker Academic, 2019), 52–55.
15. See Gorrell, *Always On*, 72–75; and O. Alan Noble, *Disruptive Witness: Speaking Truth in a Distracted Age* (Downers Grove, IL: IVP Academic, 2018), 28–30.
16. Sherry Turkle, *Alone Together: Why We Expect More from Technology and Less from Each Other* (New York: Basic Books, 2011), 284–88.

The rise of "digital church" and the individual calibration of Christianity that comes with it have their precedent in an older form of technology: televangelism. In its inception, the televised church service was seen as a way to broaden reach, to expand the scope of the preached Word to an audience isolated at home or at work or unable to come gather physically, calibrating the message to the individual viewer.[17] With the rise of digital networks, trends continue to shift away from cable channels and toward other forms of physically displaced church, but what remains is a common ethos of the time of gathering as a vehicle for *content delivery for individual listeners.*

The quiet part, in the digital age, begins to be said out loud: we view church primarily as a chance to hear, and to hear for myself. For if a sermon or worship service is the same when I hear it by myself in my living room or walking the dog as when I experience it in the physical building of the church surrounded by others, then we see that what was always happening was only a gathered group of isolated persons, persons who happened to be in the same room.

But let us leave behind the more extreme examples of digital mediation and the ways in which they make the priority of the individual more transparent to us. The more ordinary practices of the church likewise need attending to. Personal cultivation and individual hearing, seen in digital life, dominate in the ordinary practices of the church as well: being "analog" as opposed to "digital"—face-to-face instead of virtual—makes little difference, for it is the presupposition and not only the medium that matters here.

This drive (writ large by the digital revolution) to replicate nearly all of the functions of church for the individual is made possible in no small part because it is frequently as individuals that we practice our ordinary worship as well, in Scripture reading and in prayer, unwittingly cultivating habits that shift us from community and deeper into being isolated hearers and interpreters of Scripture. During the era of the Reformation, the Bible shifted in practice, from being that which was heard each week in liturgy to that which increasingly was read and discussed, leading to innovations in two different ways. First, with multiple translations emerging simultaneously, the Bible—as a

17. Quentin Schultze, *Televangelism and American Culture* (Eugene, OR: Wipf & Stock, 2003).

book—came into view not only as a decentralized authority but as a *decentralizing* authority. The prevalence of multiple translations out of Greek and Hebrew created a competition over authority concerning not only what the Scriptures *meant*, about which there was much debate, but also what the Scriptures actually *said*. The Vulgate (Latin), the Tyndale version, the Knox version, Luther's Bible: each translation produced varieties of interpretations that, while not incompatible with one another, created new centers of gravity around themselves, codified into the prayers of the church and memory of the people.[18]

The proliferation of translations came with a proliferation of new habits of reading Scripture, through Genevan school programs, Low Country German pietist reading groups, American colonial picture books, and Huguenot communities. These new habits, coupled with an increased attention to the role of the laity in church and a growing printing industry, led not to an orderly dissemination of practice but to an increasingly pluralized set of options for reading Scripture. At its utmost point, it can lead to the impression that Scripture itself encourages us to leave Scripture behind to hear the voice of God, directly calibrated to the soul. When the Scriptures are consequently taught in small groups, because the assumption is that

18. For the histories of these early translations, see Orlaith O'Sullivan, ed., *The Bible as Book: The Reformation*, (London: Oak Knoll Press, 2000); on the transformative political dimensions of these translations across Europe, see Lori Anne Ferrell, *The Bible and the People* (New Haven: Yale University Press, 2008). It is no small irony, then, that the King James Bible, though reliant on texts that were deficient from a scholarly perspective, was an attempt to rein in the plurality of translation. This was not a problem due to the proliferation of vernacular translations: as Bruce Gordon reminds us, this problem was present in critical editions of the Vulgate (Latin) as well, which were intended to preserve the unifying force of the Vulgate (as it had been under Catholicism) by clarifying its meaning but which produced variant versions that produced alternate theological readings nonetheless. "Teaching the Church: Protestant Latin Bibles and Their Readers," in *The People's Book: The Reformation and the Bible*, ed. Jennifer Powell McNutt and David Lauber (Downers Grove, IL: InterVarsity, 2017), 13–32. Attempts to work around this likewise contribute to this basic conundrum: proto-Baptist John Smyth advocated that preachers shouldn't use a printed translation at all but should translate themselves directly from Hebrew and Greek on the spot. While this prevents the issue of having a tradition formed around yet another stable translation of Scripture, Smyth ironically creates a situation where what Scripture is becomes the property not of the community but of the preacher, the one who translates it for the congregation.

Scripture and its interpretation are the property of the individual, the pedagogical process is either idiosyncratic monologues of the teacher or, conversely, an open-ended discussion of aggregate thoughts and opinions. In any event, what is emphasized is the interpretation of Scripture as the property of the individual.

Prayer, offered through what one has learned in the Scriptures, suffers accordingly. If our knowledge of God is mediated through individual readings of Scripture, then the encounter with God will follow the same pattern. Corporate prayers serve only as bookends to corporate gatherings but not as corporate offerings to God, with the implicit lesson being that prayer-as-communion with God, *real* prayer, spontaneous and never scripted by the words of others, happens when one is alone. Prayer may be done with others, but only accidentally, for one can pray only in a closet alone without loss.

The last domino to fall, then, is the moral life, for arbitration over the moral life must pass through the same grid as our reading of Scripture: the individual reader.[19] Having read and judged our Scriptures, and reinforced these readings through prayer, one may very well come to orthodox conclusions on the moral life, but as a consequence of an individualized process that makes any joint conclusions by a gathered body mostly accidental. When discussion over hard and divisive topics occurs, the conscience and individual liberty become the arbiters, without any sense of being responsible to the shared world of church, Scripture, and the God who gathers up a scattered body.[20] The individual in disagreement, already isolated and attuned to isolation as the way things are in church, simply moves on to find other like minds.

19. This is not an exclusively Protestant story within the twentieth century. See John Mahoney, *The Making of Moral Theology: A Study of the Roman Catholic Tradition* (Oxford: Clarendon, 1987), 175–223, for the unintended consequences of Vatican II's emphasis on the laity's formation of conscience, as it pertains to the rise of situation ethics and the laity's rejection of the magisterial teaching in favor of conscience.

20. Andrew Walker's *Liberty for All: Defending Everyone's Religious Freedom in a Pluralistic Age* (Grand Rapids: Brazos, 2021) is a peculiar example here, in which religious liberty for the individual is defended as a matter of divine patience, the implication being that God wills for people, prior to the eschaton, to be able to go astray in their theological convictions—as a matter of natural law! See Walker's discussions of the eschatological horizon of religious liberty in this way, built on a conviction of the inviolable value of the conscience (105–10).

In this line of dominos, one falling after another, we can observe the replication of the effects of the fall and its attendant isolation. In putting our relationship with God outside the scrutiny of others, and in elevating our consciences to a place beyond the reproach of others, we create an enclosure around ourselves that is justified by the Scriptures themselves. To return to Bonhoeffer's comment about the call of Jesus to the individual, we can now see that the call of Christ to Peter qua Peter is not the end of the journey, but the beginning. For Peter to become incorporated into Christ's body, he first has to come out of hiding behind his job, his social origins, his identity as a brother of Andrew. He will get these things back in a new form, but *only* in an altered form that has first passed through the crucible of being part of a larger body than himself.

Isolation and Church Gathering: The Temptations of the Crowds

If the temptation of the individual is one face of isolation that becomes familiar to us, the temptation of the crowd offers a different kind of temptation, but ultimately one that also perpetuates the conditions of isolation. As the phenomenon of the individual filters down through church practice, so the mentality of the crowd envelops the life of the church in analogous ways. Whereas the individualist presumption places too much on the Christian—asking them to be an excellent hermeneut, interpreter, moral authority, and arbiter—the crowd presumption takes the opposite approach (albeit toward the same end) in asking too little of the Christian. For one way forward is to embrace isolation as the cost of living in the world and to calibrate the faith to that reality. But the other way is to refuse isolation on the face and to embrace the welcoming ethos of the crowd, refusing to have a voice, a face, or gifts to offer.

The ethos of the crowd appears most clearly in the closing pages of the first chapter of *Life Together*, in which Bonhoeffer lays out the difference between the "spiritual" and "psychic" unity of groups. The "spiritual" means the work of the Holy Spirit, the union between persons that exists by Christ's mediation, while the "psychic" form of union names the logic of the crowd. By this cryptic term *psychic*, Bonhoeffer means that which is manufactured, that which is psychologically powerful but strives to create what only God can give: unity of the corporate body.[21] In Bonhoeffer's context, the dichotomy between the "psychic" and the "spiritual" versions of community would have immediately conjured up the reality of fascism: a dictator who could spellbind the people with visions of grandeur, joining them into one body created around an ideal vision of their community's place in history, was not a far-off danger. But this fascist danger was not limited to the halls of the Reichstag; it lurks in the church-community as well.

For a church culture that values the centralizing, charismatic leader, these are exceptionally strong words. But when Bonhoeffer makes such strong statements as "God hates this wishful dreaming,"[22] it is because the temptation of the crowd is an alluring one. This form of gathering, focused by the visionary leader, promises the creation of what the individual cannot have by themselves: companionship. If the condition of the individual is a more obvious problem because it places us (at best) next to one another but not *with* one another, our reasons for rejecting the crowd on these grounds are less obvious. The crowd places us next to one another, offering a common focus in experience or purpose, joining individuals in the same place, ordering individuals toward a single focus. But reckoning with the crowd forces us to consider that our common mission and experience—cherished goods of the Christian life—will not provide the basis for our common life either.

Among churches that operate as crowds, the danger of the charismatic leader who can bend the church to his (frequently "his") will is familiar to us: the moral and spiritual abuses of the strong leader are ones we need not repeat here.[23] A demagogue, though dangerous, offers a way out of individualism and isolation, providing leadership

21. Bonhoeffer, *Life Together*, 35–36. According to Bonhoeffer, this kind of community—the one united under the sway of powerful personalities or powerful slogans or attractive visions—is one that "God hates."

22. Bonhoeffer, *Life Together*, 36.

23. For two recent treatments and remedies for this phenomenon, see Scot McKnight and Laura Barringer, *A Church Called Tov: Forming a Goodness Culture That Resists Abuses of Power and Promotes Healing* (Carol Stream, IL: Tyndale Momentum, 2020); and Diane Langberg, *Redeeming Power: Understanding Authority and Abuse in the Church* (Grand Rapids: Brazos, 2020).

with vision, purpose, and meaning where individualism creates only chaos and multiplicity. The same can be said for a common mission, organizing slogan, or common experience: it promises to bind disparate people together. Yet both the demagogue and the mission only bind us *alongside* one another, not toward one another.

The crowd—organized either around a strong charismatic leader or around an ideal vision of mission or community—is dangerous precisely because it works, for a short time at least. In the end, this gathering reveals its dangerous edge. In this gathering, dreamers "enter the community of Christians with their demands, set up their own law, and judge one another and even God accordingly. . . . They act as if they have to create the Christian community, as if their visionary ideal binds the people together."[24] At stake here is the truth that the fragmentation of sin, as seen in our isolation, cannot be overcome by a sheer act of will or by an attractive personality or by a renewed mission that will galvanize us back into one body. Contemporary philosopher Alasdair MacIntyre is right when he argues that, in the end, the great temptation of modern ethics is the one presented to us by Friedrich Nietzsche: the will-to-power. Nietzsche's famous "will to power" is most readily associated with the individual, describing the ways in which an individual's character is best actualized by asserting our will over against the crowds; when we take up our isolation as a strength—an occasion to prove ourselves—we easily slip into Nietzsche's vision. But when a congregation follows the strong leader, the bureaucratic culture created around their vision simply hides the ways in which all members of the congregation are being tutored in this vision.[25]

The strong leader, the persuasive teacher, impresses on the church their scriptural hermeneutic, which in time becomes the dominant

24. Bonhoeffer, *Life Together*, 36.

25. Alasdair MacIntyre, *After Virtue: A Study in Moral Theory*, 2nd ed. (Notre Dame, IN: University of Notre Dame Press, 1984), 109–20. In what could be describing the church culture characterized above, he writes, "Whenever those immersed in the bureaucratic culture of the age try to think their way through to the moral foundations of what they are and what they do, they will discover suppressed Nietzschean premises" (114). By this MacIntyre means not that a bureaucratic structure is evil by design but that morality in these structures is ultimately inseparable from the vision of the one designing the system.

paradigm overriding all other interpretive practices, in explicit ways like sermon series and statements of faith and in subtle ways like budgetary or staffing decisions. In this, the Scripture reading, practices of worship, and structure of the church conform all wills to the one strong will, creating not a community of readers but the image of one person refracted in the ethos of many. If the individual envisions a world in which the individual's will is ultimate, the crowd surrounding the strong leader ultimately has no need for this will, for the crowd is happy to sublate the individual into its mission.

But the strong leader is not the only sign that the ethos of the crowd is at work: we must linger for a moment with the danger of the common mission statement, the diffuse counterpart to the singular charismatic leader. A mission statement, a common building campaign, or a churchwide focus on a particular goal or topic remains more flexible and forgiving than a leader whose dictates from the pulpit offer a renewing energy and unifying focus for the congregation struggling to find a common focus.

There is no prize for a church being unclear in its priorities, its confession, or its worship. But the contrast between the classic confessions of faith and the mission statement helps us to see the difference. In the creeds, the elements that are confessed draw together the canon of Scripture into one complex story, which begins with God creating and culminates with the vision of Christ's return and the life everlasting. In the Apostles' Creed, for example, the congregation confesses that they are a part of a wide-ranging work of God from creation to eschaton, and it confesses in a way that excludes heresy but creates room for disagreement about *how* that faithful confession of God in Scripture should be lived out and understood. In that complexity, there are many unspoken checkpoints—a story that passes through deserts, oceans, crosses, and tombs, all of which are important to the story of the church that confesses the Scriptures.[26]

26. This canonical confession is not one that closes down any need for further reading of Scripture, eliminating dissent, but typologically opens up Scripture's riches for future insights and discussions. In contrast to lazy accounts of the development of creeds that describe the entirety of tradition's development as purely an exercise in imperial politics, the Scripture's riches are opened up in contestation by the common frame of the creeds by which the early church demarked how the logic of the

But in mission statements, the complexity of Scripture, which gathers the diverse points up into a singular story of God, is exchanged for a singular focus on certain scriptural elements or practices that are perhaps needed at the moment: a focus on charity, grace, forgiveness. These are not bad foci to have. But congregations are more like confessions of faith than like mission statements: they are complex nodes of God's activity that are brought together into a singular and variegated story. When the story of Scripture is truncated into a mission statement, the variegated aspects of a congregational reality come to be read through one lens, a lens analogous to the interpretive singularity of the charismatic leader.

In time, the mission statement is unable to accommodate the complexity of a church-community and is best suited to a crowd in need of a binding focus. If in the individualist church isolation is celebrated under the sign of "appreciating difference," in the crowd-church isolation is rebuffed by naming that which can and cannot be borne. There will be things that find themselves "outside the vision," creating a church that cannot bear even good difference. Whereas the first kind of church makes gathering nearly obsolete, the latter kind gathers so closely, bonded by its vision, that it cannot bear the different persons and strange gifts that might threaten the unity of the vision.

As with the church afflicted by the sign of individualism, so also in the church of the crowd, other effects appear downstream. The successful crowd-church will replicate its vision, either by additional sites or by planting additional churches. The multisite church, it has been argued, is a cogent missions strategy, attuning its structural life to missional concerns; as a church gets too big, it multiplies out geographically to reach more people. But as Jonathan Leeman argues, such an ecclesiology—of one site refracted out into multiple satellites—yields decisions that cause the crowd ethos at the heart of the church simply to proliferate out into other geographies.[27] Creating

---

Scriptures unfolded. See Robert Jenson, *Systematic Theology*, vol. 1, *The Triune God* (Oxford: Oxford University Press, 1997), 23–41.

27. Jonathan Leeman, *One Assembly: Rethinking the Multisite and Multiservice Church Models* (Wheaton: Crossway, 2020), 33–34: "The multiservice model broke the connection between church and gathering. It trained Christians to view 'church' as performance for several decades, allowing the multisite model to easily, perhaps inevitably, follow just like the Internet church inevitably follows the multisite church."

a separate church with its own leadership through a church plant, born of the crowd-church, likewise leads to the same end here, for if the ones who train the planters are themselves committed to the logic of the crowd, only a crowd will follow.

It is not only single congregations that are tempted to avoid the logic of the crowd through appeal to a visionary leader or a unifying mission; traditions as a whole are susceptible to these remedies. Traditions emerge initially through the influence and formulations of key figures, but even polyphonic traditions such as Catholicism are not immune from this phenomenon, through the outsize influence of certain genius figures within a movement. Whether it is the singular accomplishment of a Thomas Aquinas—whose resurgence in the late-nineteeth century shaped the discourse of much of contemporary Catholic theology—or the judgments of the papacy, tradition alone does not provide an alternative to isolation, in that traditions as such bear the outsize markers of some key persons and not others.[28] Put more strongly, church isolation cannot be undone by appealing to the cohesiveness of tradition alone[29], to a strong leader, or to a common vision, for these exchange the prison of one's own private judgment for the judgment of another: isolation is not undone at its root in either case, for we are still hiding, only now under the words of another.[30]

28. Terrence Tilley's reminder that tradition bears the double-meaning of "handing over" (treason) and "handing down" is a useful rejoinder to the overemphasis on tradition as an anodyne to individualism. See Terrence W. Tilley, *Inventing Catholic Tradition* (Maryknoll, NY: Orbis Books, 2000), 11–13. Willie James Jennings likewise makes this point in *After Whiteness: An Education in Belonging* (Grand Rapids: Eerdmans, 2021), 45–46.

29. Traditioned thinking and action is, at one level, indispensable for Christian faith: if we are conceiving of discipleship as action over time, then it is impossible to think of the Christian life without considering it diachronically. My point here is that, taken alone, traditions can obviate the need for present judgments: traditions that are not traditioning—i.e., inducting people into a community over time—contribute to the dynamics named here.

30. There is a case to be made that submitting to the wisdom of others is right and good, and to be sure, none of us self-initiate the journey of the Christian life: all are called by God to God through the words and wisdom of another. And as such, the Christian life is never (rightly) one of our own making. But the temptation described here is one of deference, out of a fear of response that is ultimately a refusal to offer one's gifts and to speak.

In contrast to the church of the individual, the crowd-church offers shelter to the isolated, but in a different way: through being part of something larger than themselves. In the crowd, the individual joins themselves to a larger ethos and purpose, escaping the loneliness of being isolated, but does so in a way in which they will be joined only to the one articulating the vision and not to those beside them. Hiding, as Bonhoeffer acutely put it, is still happening, but the act of pulling back from God and others is now disguised: the isolated has adopted the words, interpretative vision, voice, and ethos of others, so that they will not have to offer their own gifts, words, and actions. They remain hidden, not in withdrawal, but in the anonymity of a group.

Beyond Diagnosis and toward a Therapy

It can be an act of grace when we see these dynamics of how, even when following our best intentions, we are repeating isolation, not offering an alternative to it. This is true even in "normal" times when our avenues of social life are relatively uncompromised or when our pews are full. For we think that by *being among people*, we are living within community. But it is rather simply expanding the problem: we remain not in community but among *crowds*, thus avoiding the true call to come out from among them.

But if there is one thing to be thankful to have lost in coming to the realization of what our church practices have been doing, it is perhaps this: the illusion that in many instances, when we attend church, something distinctly different is happening with respect to isolation. To be sure, we hear the words of Christ in church when we scarcely hear them anywhere else. But when we find ourselves able to replicate everything about church *without actually being gathered together as church-community*, we can graciously see that we have simply been repeating the isolation of the broken creation rather than amending it in any meaningful way.

This is the bad news, that so much energy over recent years oriented toward drawing in persons to church has amplified a fundamental effect of sin (our isolation from one another) rather than offering a different way forward. But there is a silver lining here: we can see, to the degree that it can be done, without remainder, in the absence of other people, that what we have been doing has only accidentally been about building up a *body* of Christ. And that is a gift: to never see this is to simply be caught in a cycle of doing things without ever asking *why* they are being done and to what end these practices are leading.

At this point, however, we have only identified the operations of isolation, not actually replaced them within anything. We are the proverbial house swept clean, simply waiting now for isolation to return even more strongly. And so, from here we will go on to venture a therapy away from isolation: union in Christ. This is the work that will occupy us from here on out.

Three

The Logic of
Bodily Community

In the previous chapter, we underwent a kind of ground-clearing exercise, turning the sharp light on the ordinary aspects of our church lives. Having pulled apart the ways in which church practice can perpetuate the isolation of sin, we will now explore how the church is sustained as a community in the person of Jesus Christ. For it is only when we see that it is only *ever* through Christ that we have communion with one another that we can bring back in all the good things we had to set aside in the previous chapter. In order to receive the gifts that are close, to once again take up the work of planting churches, of discipling, of baptizing and singing, we needed to first examine our practices honestly to see how they were furthering our problem rather than participating in a solution. Having briefly defined community in chapter 1—over against the individual and the crowd—we will continue naming what constitutes it and what makes it Christian.

To begin, the logic of bodily community follows from what it means to take seriously the claim that "in [Christ] all things hold together" (Col. 1:17). It is the very logic of the incarnation: that God (who is not creation) comes to us through the ways of creation, to draw all of creation to God. And so, affirming bodily communities and the desire for the presence of others is not somehow less holy, for bodily presence is entailed in the logic of salvation.[1] To be absent from one another in body as the church is the exception, and not the rule, within the economy of God's salvation. As Holy Saturday (the day of Christ's absence) exists between Friday and Sunday (the days of Christ's presence to us), so times apart from one another are to be ordered toward reunion. If we live that time in anticipation, we live it well, but if we live with absence as the norm, as the thing itself, we are missing the logic of God's activity in creation: we are meant to be bodily present to one another, as God is present corporeally to us.[2] For us to desire a different kind of economy—an invisible and pure church, akin to a friend who exists only in our memory but never in person, or a relationship that we can imagine independent of the real difficulties of skin and bone—is to desire something other than a church-community: an idol.

Why Bodily Community?

It is with no small irony that the author of many of the letters of the New Testament writes eloquently about the nature of the church while himself in prison and deprived of its presence. Paul, writing to the Philippian church, praises their gracious gifts to him,

1. Dietrich Bonhoeffer, *Life Together*, trans. Daniel W. Bloesch, in *Life Together; Prayerbook of the Bible*, Dietrich Bonhoeffer Works 5 (Minneapolis: Fortress, 1996), 29: "A human being is created as a body; the Son of God appeared on earth in the body for our sake and was raised in the body. In the sacrament the believer receives the Lord Christ in the body, and the resurrection of the dead will bring about the perfected community of God's spiritual-physical creatures. Therefore, the believer praises the Creator, the Reconciler and the Redeemer, God the Father, Son and Holy Spirit, for the bodily presence of the other Christian."

2. In *Intellectual Appetite: A Theological Grammar* (Washington, DC: Catholic University of America Press, 2009), 118–23, Paul Griffiths explores the dynamics of how we desire in absence, stating that whenever we desire something, it is always a created being, whether in the world of ideas, bodies, or experiences. But when we desire these creations, we desire them in and through God, such that to desire them rightly is to desire God through them. To desire the thing (whether it is church or another person) apart from the dynamics of flesh through which God appears is to desire an idol of our own control.

their willingness to share in his sufferings, and the ways in which their own Epaphroditus risked his own life to assist Paul. But in all of this, Paul remained physically separated from this body that he loved.

The span of our physical lives together is temporary, set not only by our mortality but by the accidents of history. The measure in which God gives the gift of gathering, whether briefly to Paul or in a more sustained fashion to those preparing for ministry or intermittently with Sunday worship and communal life, whenever it happens, is grace.[3] But the graciousness of our common life is not determined by its duration; what lasts the longest or is most commonly available cannot be confused with what is most true. Whether it happens for a few minutes for the prisoner or for years on end to the monk living among other Christians, it is a common feature to all of the Christian life, for this is how God comes to us, as the one who approaches us in our bodily limits.[4]

The logic of Christian community entails the logic of the body, insofar as what the Christian community is depends first on what Christ is. Here an important disjuncture arises, however, for the flesh that Christ shares with all other humans is both like and unlike ours: Christ is the eternal Son who takes on flesh, though flesh without the proclivities of sin.[5] The bodies that we are as humans are created in the *imago Christi*, within the contours of the incarnation of the Word, and therefore our bodily life receives its meaning and purpose within the trajectory set by Christ: toward resurrection and participation in the good that is God. Prior to resurrection, our baptism invites us into a bodily communion with God, nourished and cleansed, and into the company of Christ's gathered body, the church.

As we saw in the previous chapter, this description of God's work contrasts sharply with an account of Christianity in which what one

3. Bonhoeffer, *Life Together*, 30.
4. Bonhoeffer, *Life Together*, 31.
5. Paul J. Griffiths, *Christian Flesh* (Stanford, CA: Stanford University Press, 2018), 28. Here, Griffiths traces four contours of Jesus's own flesh—natal, damaged, transfigured, and resurrected—arguing that it is because of the resurrected character of Christ's flesh that all baptized flesh might take part of what is Christ's.

needs is fully available when we are separated from others (whether by oneself or in a crowd). The mystery of God's economy is that this world is loved into being by a God who is one with those creatures while not one of those creatures, that we are loved in time by one who is not constituted by time: in Christ, the one who took on flesh, all flesh finds its meaning together in Christ. It is in keeping with the sheer gratuity of the presence of God in and through flesh that we always receive God through other creatures of flesh, from outside our own resources, our own creaturely limits. There is no *need* for isolation from one another, in other words, to know God, for it is through and with this body of those gathered by Christ that we encounter the living God.

The nature of Christian community follows from this. God, who comes to creation, though not bound by creation, comes to heal creation in a bodily fashion, a way that is *appropriate to creation*: we are healed by God through the gathered body. It is in this light that we can now see further into Matthew 25's famous eschatological scene: the church is judged by its inability to embrace those who are the figures of their own condition, isolated and broken creatures. In this passage, judgment is rendered on those who refrained from being present to persons who are not simply outcasts but *isolated* outcasts—those in quarantine, those in prison, the untouchable poor. For to not recognize the calling of Christ in these figures is to misunderstand our *own* condition as the church: that the truth of humanity's condition and of its healing is figured in those who are isolated, broken, and alone, apart from the communion of others in diverse ways. To reject the bodily isolated is to fail to recognize ourselves and to reject the shape of our own salvation.

So much of our ministry, as we saw in chapter 2, neglects the implications of God coming in the flesh, treating our bodily presence to one another either as accidental or as a precursor to some other kind of activity that likewise forgets that we are bodily creatures who need healing of the soul and the flesh, and need it from beyond our own impoverished resources. Coming to terms with this means beginning again: recognizing that bodily presence is not an additional feature of church but inseparable from the gift of God's own self-revelation.

Union in Christ: Bodily Persons

At this point, all we have done is to affirm, with the host of Christian witnesses, that bodily presence is indispensable not only for what the church is but for the economy of God's salvation and presence to us. It is the God who takes on flesh who comes to creation and claims a visible body in the world. But what does that union of God to the world look like? What does it mean that when we are knit together as a community, it is "through Jesus Christ"?

Bonhoeffer's concept of person here is important, for the person is not only the way in which God's revelation to humanity occurs—that we encounter God not as *ideas* or *potentialities* but as *this person among creatures*. The person is also, for Bonhoeffer, the way in which Christ appears to us—not as abstract natures but as the undivided Jesus of Nazareth.[6] The importance for Bonhoeffer of this dogma lies not only with the inseparability of the human from the divine in Christ but with the subsequent impropriety of making claims about what God is or what God wills independent of encountering Christ *through persons*: we cannot, as it were, get behind God's activity into the inner mysteries of God's will but must be led forward in discipleship always by who Christ is, through the voice of God encountered in the material words of Scripture and through the needs and presence of other persons.[7]

To be a *human* person here means in part that what one is cannot be replicated and is not reducible to some other version of a common nature; there are many humans, but each human is an instantiation

6. In the student notes from his Christology lectures, "Lectures on Christology," in Dietrich Bonhoeffer, *Berlin: 1932–1933*, trans. Isabel Best and David Higgins, Dietrich Bonhoeffer Works 12 (Minneapolis: Fortress, 2009), 299–360, Bonhoeffer reframes the christological investigation away from "how" Christ was human and divine toward the primary question of "who": Christ's personhood. It is this way that we encounter Christ, as a person. Therefore, we are affected by the works of Christ as we encounter the person of Christ, not as abstracted works but through personal encounter. See in particular "Lectures on Christology," 308–10.

7. As Michael W. Mawson notes, in *Christ Existing as Community: Bonhoeffer's Ecclesiology* (Oxford: Oxford University Press, 2018), 64, "It is only through this concrete human other that God places the human person into a situation of ethical decision and obligation." The other person exceeds the limits of my self-perception, calling me to recognize that the limit of what I am calls to me from without, that I might be drawn out of my isolation and into community.

of that common nature, a person without remainder. But this means not only that each one bears their own mark of dignity, their own irreducible value, but *also*—because of a shared nature—that their personhood is inseparable from the web of relationships that differentiates them as them. There is, in other words, no bodily life that is not, by God's grace, intended to be bound to others: we are created with the nature appropriate to a human, and we stand as ourselves only as we share that common nature, that common portion of being human.[8]

Because of what we see in the person of Christ, the economy of God's revelation to us continues through this same bodily presence, through the presence of Christ at the table, through the presence of Christ in the preached Word, and through the gathered body of Christ together. We can follow the through line of Bonhoeffer's thinking: because this is how God encounters us—not as ideas but in persons who encounter us from without—the church as community is inextricable from receiving and following Christ. The way in which Christ comes to the world is thus in fact how God *continues* to guide us: in the embodied community of the church, in our confession, consolation, reading, moral challenge, and worship. It is bodily form that leads here—in the ongoing economy of Christ and Christ's body (at the table and as the church). We do not have access to whatever might be the case "behind" that: there is no escaping the difficulties of gathered bodily life in order to find the presence of God. Put differently, we do not have secret access to the inner workings of God's triune life or to the inner workings of another person's conscience or to the mysteries of God's will: we must follow where we are led by the presence of Christ, who approaches us in material forms.

Likewise, we are created not to be collections of opinions or ideas but to be persons, not to mirror the inner life of the triune God (for only God knows what it means to be God in this way) but to participate

8. In elucidating this, I rely here on Robert Spaemann, *Persons: The Difference between "Someone" and "Something,"* trans. Oliver O'Donovan (Oxford: Oxford University Press, 2006), 28–33. As Spaemann writes, commenting on the centrality of the body for the disclosure of our selves, "The body implies vulnerability to radical objectification. But it is the hallmark of personality to see in another's body the disclosure and revelation of another centre of being, to accept displacement from the central position that is determinative for all non-personal life" (80).

in that life of God in a way appropriate for creatures. To be a person is not to lose my materiality, becoming other than creaturely, but to be a human who participates in unity with others, a way that requires the reorientation of my will, my thinking, and most importantly, how I look for God. To be a *person* in this way is possible by God's own activity toward us: the one who is three persons and yet one God calls the fragments of humanity together into one body that does not obviate the creaturely distinctions but unites us into a new body of Christ's own making.

To be a community, as we saw in chapter 1, means that what we are as creatures—our will, our agency, our desire—receives a new orientation: *with* and *for* the other person, in Christ.[9] As opposed to other social entities, such as my own city, which acts occasionally as a community—committing to each other beyond particular tactical moments—the church-community is not built on commonalities or affinities. On the face, this is something that no Christian would object to: we are united by the work of God, not by what nationality we are or by who our families are. But Bonhoeffer invites us to reflect on this more deeply, in three ways. First, apart from community, we cannot have Jesus Christ. Second, we cannot belong to one another apart from Jesus Christ's mediating people to one another. And third, this union of persons in Christ is the eternal logic of who we are as creatures. When taken together, these three truths yield a profoundly grounded and creaturely picture of the Christian life.

Community through Jesus Christ

If it is Christ who reveals God, and Christ who calls together a body, then at the center of our community is Christ, who mediates us

9. As Andrew Davison indicates in *Participation in God: A Study in Christian Doctrine and Metaphysics* (Cambridge: Cambridge University Press, 2019), this definition of community builds on the notion of what the creature of God is: a being that is not self-contained but porous by design, as a facet of it having been given its existence by God, which both establishes it and requires its participation in God's gifting for the creature's life to be coherent. Creatures do not have absolute existence but subsist within God's world, which means in part that no claim to absolute autonomy can make sense for a creature given its existence (71–80).

together into one body. Because Christ's reconciliation is not just for me qua me but for me-with-others, it follows that I can never come to Christ *apart from* others. To see this, consider the structure of the Christian life. Who I am and who I am made to be come to me from outside myself: I did not give birth to myself, create myself, call myself into God's presence. Similarly, Bonhoeffer writes, God has put the words of pardon, of assurance, of God's truth, into the mouths of others so that we may hear those words coming again and again to us from beyond ourselves.[10] The will of another, lifting me up when I cannot walk, and the voice of another, praying for me when I cannot find the words to pray, are the mirror of how God comes to me: as a word breaking through and confirming my true self, despite my own introspective account of my failures.

Linking the presence of God's Word together with the challenging, comforting, frail, and confronting words of other people means that I cannot truly hear the gospel if I am not hearing it with others. This is more than a practical matter; it is a theological one: the gospel is not a word that I generate out of my own imagination but one that strikes from the outside, as the quenching of my thirst and the slaking of my hunger by the hands of another. God entrusts this work to be done in a mediated way—through the hands of others—and not in some unmediated way not only because the Word of God is true where my own conscience either judges me too harshly or not at all[11] but also because, in creation, we were not meant to be without one another before God. Humans are not a mass of individuals but a singular corpus for which there is only one truth of our union: the Word by which we have been created, Jesus Christ.

To confess this, in turn, means not only that I cannot have Christ *without* others but also that I cannot have Christ alongside *only* ones I show pity to: the sick and the prisoner. To say that I cannot have Christ without others is to say that I cannot have Christ without the stranger (whom I do not know or choose) and the enemy as well:

10. Bonhoeffer, *Life Together*, 113.
11. Bonhoeffer, *Life Together*, 33. For Bonhoeffer on the conscience, see Brian Gregor, "Bonhoeffer's 'Christian Social Philosophy': Conscience, Alterity, and the Moment of Responsibility," in *Bonhoeffer and Continental Thought: Cruciform Philosophy*, ed. Brian Gregor and Jens Zimmerman (Bloomington: Indiana University Press, 2009), 201–25.

"This love [of Christ] knows no difference among diverse kinds of enemies, except that the more animosity the enemy has, the more my love is required. No matter whether it is a political or religious enemy, they can all expect only undivided love from Jesus' followers. . . . Unhypocritically and purely we are to serve and help our enemies in all things. No offering which a lover would bring to a beloved can be too great for our enemies."[12] Once we confess that we cannot have Christ apart from others, the "others" that I am joined to are not only those whom I pity and draw into the church (those whom I might have some kind of power or sway over) but those who are stronger than me and, indeed, might be my enemies.

We need only recall that in Matthew 5, when Jesus teaches about how we worship, he says that worship cannot—indeed, *must not*—take place when someone is at odds with me (Matt. 5:23–24).[13] Being bound up with the good of my enemies, in Christ, shows me that when I chose people to be in fellowship with out of pity, I was creating a community in my own image, including people I could care for instead of my enemies and excluding those I did not want to care for. In Christ, we are in this together or not at all, given toward one another and for one another's good, weak and strong, enemies and friends together, bound only in Christ's calling.

This union that Christ brings, which cuts past all of my self-satisfaction about who is worthy to receive my good intentions, creates a missionary impulse here. It is not enough for *me* to no longer be alone, for there is no "me" apart from the "we" constituting creation: for as humanity, we are bound up together in Adam, and likewise redeemed by the one human, Christ. That we can think of multiple constituencies that are in competition with one another is an *effect* of sin, not a reality for us to accommodate church life to. The reason we can think of Christ's work in ways that are less than this all-encompassing way is that we are willing for that isolation to be displaced somewhere else, to those people who deserve the isolation from us that they experience.

A second point follows: if the church exists because of Christ, then it is only through Christ that our relations can be joined together.

<hr>

12. Dietrich Bonhoeffer, *Discipleship*, trans. Barbara Green and Reinhard Krauss, Dietrich Bonhoeffer Works 4 (Minneapolis: Fortress, 2001), 139.

13. See Bonhoeffer's commentary in *Discipleship*, 123.

This point, though, goes all the way down: not only does Christ want to draw me together to those who are most *distant* from me (my enemies), but it is only through Christ that I can be drawn together to those whom I would consider most *naturally mine*: my friends, those with whom I have common interest, my family, my spouse. If Christ is the logic of creation, then there is no natural connection that does not need mediating: there is no immediate connection between people that can stand or be sufficient.

This calls into question a most basic assumption of church organization: age and affinity groups. Most frequently, our churches simply are organized around these natural affinities of age, gender, family structure, or interests, either consciously or unconsciously. This is not to say that there is no value in social institutions or cultivating natural affinities and relationships, for two reasons. First, a church quite simply grows out of the soil in which it is planted, with the limits of demography intrinsic to it, and second, ordinary relations of family, civic sphere, and region, rightly cultivated and sustained, are part of how God preserves human society.[14] But suggesting that the relationships that are most immediate to us—whether parent to child or spouse to spouse, or nation member to nation member[15]—do not need to be mediated by Christ, in the same way that my life needs to be joined by Christ to that of a fellow Christian whom I have nothing in common with, is to insidiously suggest that there is at least one arena of human relations in which Christ's mediation is unneeded.

At a peripheral level, the implications for church organization of our only union being through Christ are legion. Age-specific ministries, which assume that what people need most is mentoring with like-minded peers, are to be employed as the exception and not the rule; building a church on common interests or "stages of life" is

14. For this discussion, see Bonhoeffer's essay "The Concrete Commandment and the Divine Mandates," in *Ethics*, trans. Reinhard Krauss, Charles C. West, and Douglass W. Stott, Dietrich Bonhoeffer Works 6 (Minneapolis: Fortress, 2005), 388–408.

15. On this point, Benedict Anderson's caveats of nations as effectively "imagined" is instructive. It is not the case that "nations" are naturally occurring relations like genetic families; rather, they do possess imaginative sway over us, and those imagined relations among nation members, over time, become seen as "natural." See Benedict Anderson, *Imagined Communities: Reflections on the Origin and Spread of Nationalism* (New York: Verso Books, 1991), 39–49.

revealed to be organizing our churches as crowds, organized around like interests (willing alongside one another). Even the married—those in the most intimate relation of all—do not have each other directly, but only in Christ, so that we may love our spouses as they are in Christ and not as we wish them to be, and as such should not *prima facie* be separated off in our organizational life.[16] While we might think of family bonds as outside this discussion—that family bonds are social ones that we might wish to tacitly defend on natural law grounds—such a vision is the same that would lead us to think a church might indeed be built on some other natural affinity, such as race or nationality, without issue.[17] The point, then, is not whether the family structure exists as something to be defended or indeed whether families bring up additional pastoral concerns; the question is whether, in trying to nurture the family, the family structure has been isolated from needing the same mediation by Christ as all other human relations.

The central target here is the assumption we have come to hold that our connection to others is immediate: that we can connect with others intimately and truly apart from the healing work of God. The desire to connect directly apart from the work of God is a false turn in the road, a lingering habit from wanting to overcome our distance between one another apart from having God bind us together. When we refuse this more innocent face of the desire for immediacy, a more pernicious dimension is likewise set aside: the desire to be able to remake the world in our own image instead of having the world and all that it is in it be given to us only through Christ. When there exists a group that is not knit together with Christ at the center, there is only a group of individuals in whom the most persuasive, most

16. Bonhoeffer, *Life Together*, 43: "Spiritual love, however, comes from Jesus Christ; it serves him alone. It knows that it has no direct access to other persons. Christ stands between me and others."

17. Here, the Orthodox ecclesiological conception of *symphonia*, the integration of the church into a region or ethnicity, must be put into question—not only because what occurs in this form tends toward ethnonationalism but because it presumes that the work of the renewing Word in the church builds on "natural" bonds of locality. It is this presumption of the unity of geographic and ethnic localities as the material grounds upon which the church is organized that becomes a problem. See Cyril Hovorun's analysis in *Political Orthodoxies: The Unorthodoxies of the Church Coerced* (Minneapolis: Fortress, 2018), 147–76.

powerful, or most abusive will inevitably rule the group.[18] It is only when all persons have Christ as the way that they come together that the weak and the strong can be in the same group, that parents do not exasperate their children (Eph. 6:4), that children do not over- whelm or abuse their parents (Eph. 6:2; Matt. 15:1–9), and that the opinions of the most charismatic do not overpower the voices of the timid (1 Cor. 12:24–26). Absent this mediation of Christ, human sociality becomes the face of an individual writ large by power. But it is only with Christ that the face of a community appears, through the multitudes of the body of Christ gathered by the Spirit.

Community in Christ Jesus

The second dimension of this community, Bonhoeffer writes, is that it is a community not only through Jesus Christ (mediated together only by Jesus) but also *in* Jesus Christ.[19] By this he means that it is a community that finds itself shaped and ordered by Jesus Christ. At first glance, this seems to be a very low bar: What church doesn't call itself shaped by Jesus Christ, the revelation of God, the Holy One? If Christ is the one who comes to the community in creation, drawn together over time through the world, then the community that is shaped in Christ would not try to disavow their creaturely shape, wishing for a very different shape or a very different disciple- ship than the one that comes to them in time, asking why another disciple might be called to live until Christ returned but not them (John 21:20–22).

The danger of self-selection for the church appears here: that of *re- jecting* the world into which one has been placed, seeking release from the isolation of sin by abandoning one's neighbors to it, rejecting the grounded call that has been given. A generation raised on the "church versus culture" distinction of H. Richard Niebuhr was wrongly lulled into thinking that there was somehow a way for churches to remain distinct from culture, when in fact churches are themselves kinds of culture, permeated and interwoven with the world around them all the

18. Bonhoeffer, *Life Together*, 45–46.
19. Bonhoeffer, *Life Together*, 31.

time.[20] Because we are creatures, traversing the world between Adam and Christ, the isolation of the world is already inside the building: the question is one of *what to do* with that isolation.

The creaturely nature of the church means that certain creaturely marks are peculiar to any church, some of which may be embarrassing to a church that wishes it corresponded more directly to a vision it had for itself. If a church draws predominantly from millennials in an area populated by millennials, or predominantly white, middle-class persons in a predominantly white, middle-class area, this is who God has placed the church among, even if the conditions of this homogeneity are rightly to be challenged.[21] While we must not despise the ways in which Christ draws particular communities, this attention to the goodness of particularity is also an opportunity to see how that demographic particularity is the result of isolation having been made into law and legislation, forcing a false "naturality" on the world. To hate the world into which the church has been born is, in some very real ways, to dismiss the world one has been given to live in: Bonhoeffer's own response to the Nazis in helping organize a new seminary outside the German Evangelical Church was not an abstracted response to "evil" but an action intended to amend a very specific wrong against the church in Germany.

To bring it back to our discussion here, to be brought together in Christ is to receive the form of Christ's giving, whether homogeneous or diverse, well attended or sparsely attended. The temptation here is not so much that the church is composed of those around it—and indeed, reflects the world around it—but that it *resents* that form, wishing for its gathering to be something else.

The pressure for a church to reflect an idealized reality is, in fact, a pressure to reject the flesh and blood that God has given around us

20. Kathryn Tanner, critiquing Niebuhr in *Theories of Culture: A New Agenda for Theology*, Guides to Theological Inquiry (Minneapolis: Fortress, 1997), rightly notes that "Christian identity simply cannot be secured by a sharp cultural boundary" (108), but rather "boundaries are determined, in sum, by how a Christian way of life is situated within a whole field of alternatives" (111).

21. To say, for example, that white people need Jesus is not incompatible with saying that there are historically malicious reasons behind white people living in predominately the same parts of town. See Richard Rothstein, *The Color of Law: A Forgotten History of How Government Segregated America* (New York: Liveright, 2018).

in favor of an abstraction more suited to our vision. To be clear: this is not to dismiss aspiration or change—it is right and good to hope and pray that God changes the church, including the ways the church's structure has caused it to see cultural divisions of race and class as "natural," explaining away historic racism as cultural dynamics or "natural separation." But to jump over the frailties in front of us is to miss the ways in which Christ has called the church to embrace the ground beneath its feet.

To illustrate this, let me provide a fairly mundane example from Bonhoeffer's own life. Bonhoeffer worked for over a decade in various contexts as a youth minister, ministering to the numerous youth surrounding the church in Spain, England, and Germany. To neglect ministry to the young would have been wrong, but what Bonhoeffer finally found himself at odds with was that the way youth ministry was constructed simply repeated the divisions that the world traded on. The way forward was neither to jump to more glamorous ecumenical or pastoral work, nor to adopt the modality of youth ministry that treated the youth as a separated culture from that of adults, but to attend to the many youth who were in the church as a result of the culture being what it was, and to do the hard work of drawing them into the gathered body instead of dividing them off from the rest of the body.[22]

Community in Christ Jesus *Eternally*

We give attention to these first two dimensions because of the third: that this community that is not of my making—of persons together united in a way that refuses the isolation that our society simply takes for granted—is the design of God. Put differently, how we are called together as church is what we are to be always: "But if we have been elected and accepted with the whole church in Jesus Christ before we could know it or want it, then we also belong to Christ in eternity with one another. We who live here in community with Christ will

---

22. For Bonhoeffer's theses on youth ministry, see "Theses on Youth Work in the Church," in *Berlin: 1932–1933*, 515–18. For a full analysis of this aspect of Bonhoeffer's ministry, see Andrew Root, *Bonhoeffer as Youth Worker* (Grand Rapids: Baker Academic, 2014).

one day be with Christ in eternal community."[23] In this point, we are directed to the ultimate stakes of the shape of our church: if it is of Christ, and if Christ is the one in whom all creation hangs together, then the life together we share now as one body will continue beyond death. The form the church bears now is its intended form before God forever. We are not called, in other words, to bear each other's burdens and live as one person now, only to be liberated from this vocation in eternity, standing before God as individuals once more, or as something other than creatures.[24] Rather, the shape of our living now as a community of persons *is* the shape of our communion with God: our eschatological life is not an effacement of our creatureliness but its fullness. To refuse the gift of Christ's shaping of a community now *is* to refuse it in the hereafter; to embrace the intoxicating power of isolation here is to never have known the Christ who comes to overcome the power of sin now and forever.

The implications of this with respect to our knowledge of God in eternity are dazzling in and of themselves: that we worship God eternally not as aggregated individuals but as a body together—that our worship is that of an interdependent body. But the temporal stakes here are just as high: our existence as a church now is as a sacrament, a participation of creation in the gift of God in Christ. Cast in this light, the fight against isolation and the refusal to capitulate to its logic are nothing less than a fight against the principalities and exalted powers! Death itself, Scripture teaches, appears to us through many guises and is behind manifold sin, and likewise, isolation never confronts us directly but in many attractive faces and plans. Viewing the church not simply as an optional feature of the Christian life but as the very staging ground of our eternal existence before God gives

23. Bonhoeffer, *Life Together*, 33. As Andrew Davison puts it, "If human beings are inherently social creatures, then perfection of happiness ought to pertain not only to the end, which is the apprehension and enjoyment of God, but also to the manner, or mode, which we might expect to be a humanly social one" (*Participation in God*, 124). See also Germain Grisez, "The True Ultimate End of Human Beings: The Kingdom, Not God Alone," *Theological Studies* 69 (2008): 38–61.

24. The tradition of the beatific vision, the perception of God as God, does not mitigate the distinction of creatures and God—seeing God's essence as God knows this—but emphasizes the ability of creatures to see God in ways appropriate for us as creatures, christologically mediated and calibrated. See Hans Boersma, *Seeing God: The Beatific Vision in Christian Tradition* (Grand Rapids: Eerdmans, 2018).

new importance not only to our gathered life but also to how we strive against isolation in all its forms.

In joining in this form of the church now, we are being bound up together into a body that journeys together and that will exist in Christ together into eternity. This kind of church—which we are being trained in now—is bound up with suffering, but not so that I might become exemplary in my care for the suffering out of pity: this would again isolate me from the church as an untouchable exemplar. The union we have with one another, in bearing one another's burdens, is to be joined together into the shape of the one who suffers and mediates for the world.[25] In joining in the way of Christ, I find others who are likewise joined to Christ. They will not be, as we see in the Gospels, the ones whom I would have chosen by nature or by affinity as my companions: Matthew, a former tax collector, now journeys alongside Simon the Zealot, who would have devoted himself to the destruction of all collaborators with Rome.

The confession of Hebrews, that we find ourselves in our struggles surrounded by a "great . . . cloud of witnesses" (12:1), has traditionally been understood to be nothing less than an affirmation of this kind: that the church is composed of those living on earth, the not-yet-living, and those who are living more fully than we can imagine.[26] Indeed, because of the presence of the Spirit among the church, our lives as a community are already caught up together with those of the saints. And so the stakes of our church communion are high because we are knit together with a body that is present among us, in glory, and waiting yet to be: our practice is not only a response of faithfulness to God's present work but a reception of the gifts of the past and a promise to the future.

25. Bonhoeffer, *Discipleship*, 90: "Christ suffers as vicarious representative for the world. Only his suffering brings salvation. . . . The community of Jesus Christ vicariously represents the world before God by following Christ under the Christ."

26. Richard Kidd describes this as the "strangeness" of the Christian life, in which the one who animates our common life together is simultaneously strange to creation as God: our present life is not immanentized, but made eccentric by the presence of God, eschatologically present in our timeliness. Paul S. Fiddes, Brian Haymes, and Richard Kidd, *Baptists and the Communion of the Saints* (Waco: Baylor University Press, 2014), 60–63.

A Conclusion in Transit

Writing on the Sermon on the Mount, Bonhoeffer argues that Jesus's teachings do not depict a reality awaiting us at the edge of history but instead offer the way of the cross—the way of freedom from sin and its isolation—as a present and costly reality in the world.[27] This way of Jesus is best thought of as a kind of doorway: one steps into the way of Jesus by taking the teachings of the Sermon seriously, but it is only once one enters in that we understand what that life entails.[28] But this reality, this offer of a new world, is not one that will be had by simply claiming the mediating work without the *way* of Jesus: the two are bound up together as they follow together. The disciple is led into truthfulness, into nonretribution, into forgiving enemies, and into suffering evil from the world, for it is here that they find a renewed *community*, a community in Jesus, and leave the vicious habits of isolation behind. In the truth of Jesus, we leave behind the need to defend ourselves; in the peace of Jesus, we leave behind the fear of losing our possessions or our name; in forgiving, we leave behind the fear of being shamed by the world and learn to embrace even our enemies. In each case, what is left behind is the fortress mentality of preserving one's self, for we were always ever meant to be opened up toward one another in Christ.

One of the most devastating elements of isolation is that we not only take to it so easily but also learn to love and need the vicious habits that come with it. At first, I despair of being alone, and then I learn how to cope with it by building up ways of being alone: ensuring my name, my place in the public square, my reputation. Over time,

27. Bonhoeffer, *Discipleship*, 53–56.

28. Agnes Callard, *Aspiration: The Agency of Becoming* (Oxford: Oxford University Press, 2019), best captures this dynamic when she writes that we are not changed morally by identifying the values we want to adopt, for we can have no way of knowing in advance what it looks like to be that kind of person. Rather, she argues, we begin through adopting partial habits, with additional supporting habits coming alongside as we begin to learn experientially the demands of being the kind of person we aspire to be. Callard suggests that instead of the focus on being the kind of person we should, aspiration offers its own entryway toward a changed life that we cannot yet envision, even if we have exemplars—those exemplars changed according to their own time and place, which is not ours. Likewise, the way of discipleship is one in which we enter in, not knowing what we are entering into or what it will mean to be a part of a community that bears out this new life.

this condition takes the name of "natural," the way things are.[29] But what we must unapologetically see is that this isolation—and all of the competitive, fearful ways that ensure my existence over against others—is anything but natural. For what is meant to be ours by nature as creatures of God is not fear or separation but love and communion.

Having established how isolation permeates our church practice and what difference being joined in Christ makes for this question of isolation, we are now in a position to begin looking at our theological therapy. Next we will begin to examine the dimensions of church practice, looking for ways of reconstruction away from isolation toward communion. The pattern of the next four chapters broadly follows the pattern of *Life Together*, but it does not repeat them: as noted already, to reject the contours of one's own time and place is to not wish for the church, Christ's body, but for the idea of the church, a vision of pure community that does not need to be healed.

We will turn first to the renewal of our common life (chap. 4), which serves to contextualize the ways in which our personal lives are not abolished by this turn to the community but given their right orientation (chap. 5). When we see the context of our interpersonal lives, knit together by God in ways that turn from our isolation, we can see how the ministry of Christ's body shapes and sustains this common life (chap. 6), and we can finally turn toward the ways in which this fragile communion with one another is sustained (chap. 7).

Onward.

---

29. How to name that which is given in creation—"nature"—remains a vexing question for Christian theology, semantically, ethically, and doctrinally. Here, I am suggesting that what is to be avoided is an elision of prima facie realities with doctrinal truths, when what appears to our senses is at the same time a real apprehension of the world and a corruption of creation by sin. "Natural" thus becomes a way to beatify that which remains corrupted prior to its renewal eschatologically, leading us in turn to make claims on the world that are ultimately claims of power over the world. Michel Foucault's description in *Discipline and Punish: The Birth of the Prison* (New York: Vintage, 1979), 27, remains apt on this point: "That power and knowledge directly imply one another; that there is no power relation without the correlative constitution of a field of knowledge, nor any knowledge that does not presuppose and constitute at the same time power relations." The fragmentary mode of the knowledge of other beings, as Bonhoeffer would put it, leads us to an overarching strategy of possession of another, a strategy whose goal is that our power over them and our fragmentary knowledge would then coincide.

PART TWO

THE NEW WORLD
OF CHRISTIAN
COMMUNITY

Four

Renewing Common Life

As we begin to meditate on the common life of the church and its practices, a word of warning is in order. Lauren Winner, in her provocative *The Dangers of Christian Practice*, offers this counsel:

> Sometimes damage is so obviously intrinsic to the damaged thing—so clearly proper to it—that it seems impossible to imagine the thing itself without the damage. Consider *kintsugi*—the Japanese art form wherein broken pottery is put back together with powdered gold and lacquer, highlighting, rather than trying to disguise, the fact that the bowl was broken, on the theory that the golden veins, and the history of brokenness, make the bowl more beautiful than it was before. . . . What are we to say about damages—those now-golden cracks and fissures—that are delightful to us?[1]

Winner here offers an important word of caution: if we turn toward Christian practices as a kind of fail-safe against the acids of the modern world, we will be sorely disappointed. Sometimes the damage to

---

1. Lauren Winner, *The Dangers of Christian Practice: On Wayward Gifts, Characteristic Damage, and Sin* (New Haven: Yale University Press, 2018), 7. Winner discusses the ways in which historically all of these practices bear within them the possibility for abuse, that it is not that the practice has been distorted but that the practice itself wobbles, yet God works through it nonetheless.

our Christian life comes from outside, from malign intentions, from overzealous Pharisees. But sometimes it is the practice itself that bears its own dangers: prayer can become an occasion for idolatry, Communion an opportunity to exclude those we would rather not eat with, baptism a way to reaffirm family and ethnic ties rather than transfigure them.

Yet it is through these frail practices that we as humans do that God works. As Winner concludes, "Sometimes damaged gifts lead not only to damage. And so we carry on with them, always hoping that, despite the damage, they will return us to one another, and to the Lord."[2] Saint Augustine, when describing sin, describes it like overcoming a wound: it is important not only to stop the spread of the sickness but also to reverse the damage of the injury.[3] Christ, in other words, is not only the one who overcomes death but also the one who undoes the damage done to creation. And so it is with our own healing here from isolation.

It is not enough, as we saw, to say that the individual is mediated by Christ to God the Father, without saying that we are mediated to one another as Christ's body and embedded within creation. Our healing by Christ is comprehensive, involving the totality of what we are as creatures: related to God, to one another, and to creation. Addressing isolation, thus, must account for this complex relation, not sacrificing some aspect of what we are. Not only must our practices come to terms with the ways they enable us to hide from God, to build lives independent of God or the entanglement with others; they must also come to terms with the ways in which we hide from one another, even in the familiarity of churchgoing. What is depicted here is best understood as the formation of habit, not the erecting of architecture. To be sure, habits function best within certain environments: it is difficult to learn to cook, for example, in the bathroom as opposed to the kitchen. But it would be a mistake to see habits as

2. Winner, *Dangers of Christian Practice*, 165.
3. Augustine, *On Christian Teaching*, trans. D. W. Robertson Jr. (Upper Saddle River, NJ: Prentice-Hall, 1997), 15: "Just as a cure is the way to health, so also this Cure received sinners to heal and strengthen them. And just as physicians when they bind up wounds do not do so haphazardly but neatly so that a certain beauty accompanies the utility of the bandages, so the medicine of Wisdom by taking on humanity is accommodated to our wounds."

a kind of "technique," as opposed to the formation of movements of the soul fostered by regular forms of discipline.

In chapter 2, we introduced some of the ways in which church practice further facilitates our isolation. Once we become aware of isolation as an ingrained habit, as the normal course of our actions, thoughts, and framing of the world, how do we do differently? The good news, as I indicated earlier through Augustine, is this: insofar as the church is bound up with the world, the healing begins not as a matter of disavowing creaturely life but as learning to inhabit the world differently. Though Bonhoeffer diverges from Augustine at numerous points theologically, they concur in this: the church and world have no way of disentangling themselves, and this is, for Bonhoeffer, a gracious gift of God.

Writing from prison about this interconnection, Bonhoeffer notes that "Christ is [not only] the center and power of the Bible, of the church, of theology, but also of humanity, reason, justice, and culture."[4] In saying this, Bonhoeffer recalibrates Lutheran "two kingdoms" thinking, placing the redeeming work of Christ in the center of creation so that not only does Christian discipleship—including the redemption of isolation—have meaning for all creation but also the way home to Christ is found through the folds of the world. Christ has come to provide not a common life that is divided from society but one that will stand in the center of the village and renew not only the church but also the village and all the countryside.[5] But before turning to the ways in which Christ redeems the whole of creation, we must first do the work in house.[6] In this chapter, we

4. Dietrich Bonhoeffer, *Ethics*, trans. Reinhard Krauss, Charles C. West, and Douglass W. Stott, Dietrich Bonhoeffer Works 6 (Minneapolis: Fortress, 2005), 341.

5. Dietrich Bonhoeffer, *Letters and Papers from Prison*, trans. Isabel Best, Lisa E. Dahill, Reinhard Krauss, and Nancy Lukens, Dietrich Bonhoeffer Works 8 (Minneapolis: Fortress, 2010), 282.

6. Dietrich Bonhoeffer, *Sanctorum Communio: A Theological Study of the Sociology of the Church*, trans. Reinhard Krauss and Nancy Lukens, Dietrich Bonhoeffer Works 1 (Minneapolis: Fortress, 1996), 146–47: "In Christ, humanity really is drawn into community with God, just as in Adam humanity fell. And even though in the one Adam, there are many Adams, yet there is only one Christ. For Adam is 'representative human being' but Christ is the Lord of his new humanity. . . . While the old humanity consists of countless isolated units—each one an Adam—that are perceived as a comprehensive unity only through each individual, the new humanity

will attend to the practices of the church's gathering, to offer a vision of practices that are familiar to us but reframed with the danger of isolation now in view.

Having seen how we are joined in Christ, as well as the ways in which our practices fail to bear this out, we have described the first half of the cure according to Augustine: how Christ stops the corruption of sin from spreading. Our attention now turns in this second half to the ways in which Christ undoes the poison. This requires attending to the intimate dynamics of the body of Christ, attending to the wounds that are already there.[7] For if isolation is the harbinger of death and sin, then the temptation to abandon gathering with the body of Christ will always be present, and with it the way that our isolation is drawn out of us. But if it is through joining ourselves with Christ's body—the gathered and worshiping church—that Christ brings us to health, we must learn how to do this, aware that the temptation to withdraw and separate is always present.

Redeeming Communities, Redeeming Time

As we begin, let us start with the biggest scope and work inward, seeing the work of renewing our common life in Christ as the gathered church as implicating the whole of creation. Frequently, in patristic theology, Paul's analogy of the great exchange between Christ and Adam was employed in a narrative manner, to show how Christ's redemption of the world took place not abstractly but in a manner that redeemed the lost history of sin. To quote from Irenaeus of Lyon,

> But if the former [Adam] was taken from the dust, and God was his Maker, it was incumbent that the latter also, making a recapitulation

---

is entirely concentrated in the one single historical point, Jesus Christ, and only in Christ is it perceived as a whole. . . . I know myself to be in a guilty solidarity with the other person, but my service to the other person springs from the life principle of vicarious representative action."

7. I am borrowing this language from Mary McClintock Fulkerson, *Places of Redemption: Theology for a Worldly Church* (Oxford: Oxford University Press, 2007), 12–18, a work in ecclesial ethnography in which she describes pathologies within congregational life as "wounds" that we trace backward from the exhibited symptoms to the real issues vexing a congregation's life.

in Himself, should be formed as man by God, to have an analogy with the former as respects His origin. . . . It was necessary, therefore, that the Lord, coming to the lost sheep, and making recapitulation of so comprehensive a dispensation, and seeking after His own handiwork, should save that very man who had been created after His image and likeness, that is, Adam, filling up the times of His condemnation, which had been incurred through disobedience.[8]

When we take Paul's claim that "in Christ, there is a new creation" (2 Cor. 5:17) as the logic of salvation, then describing salvation as a renewal of individual action that does not *at the same time* take up the redemption of the social body becomes an accommodation to isolation rather than a fight against it. If salvation is first and finally a redemption of creation, then the church's work can do nothing less than mirror that.

In this way, Bonhoeffer begins *Life Together* with the most comprehensive scope: by meditating on how Christ redeems time itself.[9] The significance here is to see, from the outset, that our lives are not just a litany of activities to be accomplished but an ordering of time that must be reclaimed. Time can be narrated in numerous ways: from August to May for students, from March to March for accountants, in quarters for small businesses. Likewise, Christians for centuries have narrated time in a certain way, for it is in naming the flow of time that we name the reality of the world: creation's most significant ordering comes from Easter to Easter, not quarter to quarter. In Benedictine monasticism, for example, the day is organized according to times of worship and prayer and work; likewise, Bonhoeffer provides an account of our time together, with this end in mind: reclaiming the

8. Irenaeus, *Against Heresies* 4.22–23, in *The Apostolic Fathers with Justin Martyr and Irenaeus*, vol. 1 of *The Ante-Nicene Fathers*, ed. Alexander Roberts and James Donaldson (repr., Peabody, MA: Hendrickson, 1999), 454–55. For the resonances of Irenaeus in Bonhoeffer, see Barry Harvey, "The Body Politic of Christ: Theology, Social Analysis, and Bonhoeffer's Arcane Discipline," *Modern Theology* 13 (1997): 319–46.

9. Dietrich Bonhoeffer, *Life Together*, trans. Daniel W. Bloesch, in *Life Together; Prayerbook of the Bible*, Dietrich Bonhoeffer Works 5 (Minneapolis: Fortress, 1996), 48: "The Old Testament day begins on one evening and ends with the sundown of the next evening. That is the time of expectation. The day of the New Testament church begins at sunrise in the early morning. . . . But on early Easter morning Christ emerged victorious from the grave."

way in which time—and with it, our world—has been ordered, and doing it in a way that draws the members of the body together.

But as in Benedict's Rule, the redemption of time is not a sectarian redemption, a shifting of the church out of the world. Commenting on Benedictine life, Rowan Williams reminds us that the emphasis here is not on stability or peaceableness of the Christian life for its own sake, but as a by-product of other practices, a peaceableness that is a reworking of those things the monastery shares with its surrounding world: "Monastic life, like Christian life overall, is a form of life that depends on people having chosen it. It makes an offer, a proposal, to its society. What if this kind of life were possible after all? That's what the Church, the monastery, and many other kinds of intentional community are trying to say. What if stability, honesty and so on were indeed for all of us the basis of human life together?"[10]

Though works like Benedict's Rule, the Rule of Saint Augustine, and *Life Together* were written for communities of ministers living together to intentionally learn what it means to be the body of Christ, Williams reminds us that the aim in our life together is nothing short of the renewal of all creation, of family units, of other communities of practice, and most directly, of church life. The world is composed of numerous small communities, and for creation to be renewed, the church must be involved in renewing each of these in its own way.[11] Christ is at the center of the world, with the church at the center of Christ's work throughout all the radiant dimensions of creation; what happens as people inhabit the life together of the church fans out for the renewal of all kinds of communities, as isolation's long shadow is repealed.

It is thus not only a matter of explicitly stating our doctrine concerning what the church is; the *habits* of our gathering—of singing, praying, working, and reading Scripture—are changed. For when we turn to the days in which we live separate from one another, falling back into isolation is easy; unless these acts become movements

---

10. Rowan Williams, *The Way of St. Benedict* (London: Bloomsbury Continuum, 2020), 29.

11. Bonhoeffer, *Life Together*, 52: "Daily morning worship will take as many forms as there are communities. When a community living together includes children, it needs a different sort of daily worship than a community of seminarians."

within the soul, we will neither yearn for our lives together nor see our times separated from one another as any real loss. But if cultivated and ingrained into the practice of communities, these habits emanate out into the days in which we are scattered into the world.[12]

In this chapter, we will describe the common practices of the Christian corporate gathering as the church, but describe them in ways that allow us to see how they habituate us to a different understanding of the self than one of the individual. For the disciplines of our church gathering are meant to be vehicles by which the fragmentation of sin is undone by the remaking of the grain of our gathered life, of the body in which we know Christ, of the revelation of God, and of our journey together with that Christ. At the heart of these proposals is this: the practices of the church are not simply those activities we perform as duties but those sites of God's renewing work in our lives. As Rowan Williams describes it, "Jesus is not only someone who exercises hospitality; he *draws out* hospitality from others."[13]

12. While what follows involves structural and habitual change, this is not a churchly version of Richard Thaler and Cass R. Sunstein's *Nudge: Improving Decisions about Health, Wealth, and Happiness* (New York: Penguin, 2009), in an important way. *Nudge* operates from the assumption of privation, that altering choices toward desirable outcomes is a matter of structurally depriving people of the worst options so that they, of their own free will, choose a better option. The problem of self-interest is dealt with not by giving it a proper channel but by suppressing it in technocratic fashion. What is offered here does not begin from a presumption of self-interest, with people choosing activities to actualize that self-interest but instead builds on the activities that the community already shares, altering the way in which these activities occur toward a new habit. For a more recent criticism of the science behind such works as *Nudge*, see Jason Blakely, *We Built Reality: How Social Science Infiltrated Culture, Politics, and Power* (Oxford: Oxford University Press, 2020), 81–85.

13. Rowan Williams, *Being Christian: Baptism, Bible, Eucharist, Prayer* (Grand Rapids: Eerdmans, 2014), 42. Williams here is describing sacraments, sites of Christ's presence, and their effect on the Christian in that through these activities, we are encountering Christ. Without wading into the arguments surrounding the sacraments and their number, what is important for our purposes in the following description is that the shape of our gathered life, if we are the body of Christ gathered, follows the logic of the sacraments: our processes of life together are sacramental. There is a way of flattening sacramental language into history, as in John Howard Yoder, "Sacrament as Social Process: Christ the Transformer of Culture," in *The Royal Priesthood: Essays Ecclesiastical and Ecumenical* (Scottdale, PA: Herald, 1998), 359–73. What should be apparent thus far in what I have offered, however, is that history is not coterminous with God's presence; rather, it is through history and the bodily life

Reading Scripture, Remaking the World

The redemption of our living begins and ends with God, and it is through the Scriptures that we come to know the God who approaches us in the world. And so, to begin our rehabilitation from isolation, we begin with how we read the Scriptures and how they frame the day together. For whatever is the frame of the day is what orders the day: if it is activities ordered around sustaining our lives or around preparing for work, the day and its activities become ordered toward that as well.

If the first thing a church does is offer a time of greeting, it signals that our time together will be initiated by and return to fellowship for its own sake. To be clear, the value of friendship is increasingly denigrated and diminished, at least in industrialized societies, and churches must cultivate noninstrumental relationships of joy and virtue. But ecclesiologically, friendship and delight in the presence of others in church are not the starting point of our gathering, or even its telos: we do not gather for the sake of gathering—that, as we have been describing, is the logic of the crowd. As Samuel Kimbriel puts it, friendship, properly speaking, is that which leads us upward through the community to God, so that we become friends through God's friendship with us: our relation to one another is given most fully in this union.[14]

Consider this analogy from the rest of our week: The family, once ordered in the start of its day around survival and work, then builds its common life around the frame of shared labors of the day—shared calendars for pickups and drop-offs of children, work obligations, checking email, catching up on news that might alter our plans or occupy our worries. And so, from the beginning of the day, we repeat

---

together of the people that Christ redeems the world. For the criticism of Yoder's theology as immanentizing sacramental language, see Paul Martens, *The Heterodox Yoder* (Eugene, OR: Wipf & Stock, 2012), who concludes by arguing that "Yoder seems to leave us with a Jesus who has become merely an ethico-political paradigm that opens the door for a supersessive secular ethic" (142).

14. Samuel Kimbriel, *Friendship as Sacred Knowing: Overcoming Isolation* (Oxford: Oxford University Press, 2014), 58–66. It is this that precludes us from retreating into the interior to have something that is "ours," for if we belong to one another on the basis of what we have in Christ, then "not all that is interior is one's own" (81).

the curse, focused on extracting our livelihood from the world rather than letting our work—and the organized community of the family—be first infused by the praise of God that positions our work. Likewise, when church begins with the "time of greeting," our time together is framed by the expectation and yearning toward more of this, when it is only within a different frame that our commonalities and concerns and joy for the presence of others make sense. These two ways of beginning our time together—with friendship versus with the Scriptures—may seem to form an innocent contrast, but what we are concerned with here is the underlying presupposition of what our gatherings are.

Concern for how we begin our time together—whether with a time of greeting or with Scripture—seems a fairly innocuous example. But it reflects an ecclesiological choice about how to frame our gathered time: the gathered body/individual for their own sake (the logic of the crowd) or the Scriptures that invite us into a shared world (the logic of community). These stakes are raised, however, when it comes to how we read Scripture.

To see how these divergent assumptions—observed first in how we begin our time of gathering—are borne out in our reading of Scripture, let us consider the example of the Psalms. The Psalms, perhaps more than any other part of Scripture, encapsulate the full range of human emotion, from rage to grief to joy to bewilderment. And it is for that reason that when we read the Psalms, we are tempted to read them as that which coheres to our feelings: if I read of the psalmists' despair, I think of my own despair, and if I read of the psalmists' joy, I think of my own.

But reading in this way emphasizes the presumption that what is central to our reading of Scripture is how it speaks to our (singular) experience, such that when our desires are mismatched to the psalms read—or, by extension to other Scriptures, when our desires are mismatched to the seriousness of the law, the zeal of Jephthah, the anguish of Paul, or the joy of Mary—we look for ways to apply the Scripture to our own individual situation anyway. *I do not feel the joy of Mary, but look at how this makes a difference in my own gratitude,* one might think. This, simply put, is the presupposition of the church of the individual: that Scripture (and the church) exist to form me more into my own self.

In this mode above, though the Psalms are read corporately, they are heard by a crowd, looking to the Scriptures to cultivate a sense of self first. But consider this alternative: instead of matching our feelings to the Psalms, we let the Psalms (or whatever Scripture is read) invite us out of ourselves and offer to be the shape of our feelings, so that we contemplate joy or grief when we have none in the moment. This approach—that the Scriptures are not first for us to identify with but for us to be identified—is made possible if we know that Christ addresses us through the Scriptures. The reframing is not a way of diminishing our ability to connect with the Scriptures emotionally: far from it! Rather, this guides us to let our passions be shaped according to the things of Scripture rather than assuming that our intuitive emotional responses are apt guides to navigating our church life.[15]

As Bonhoeffer provocatively argues, in the Psalms, Christ is praying for the congregation and inviting us to join his prayer.[16] As the Word made flesh, Christ leads the church in praying this prayer book of Israel; when we consider then Christ's prayers, we are led into what we should pray for and, indeed, invited out of ourselves to join in sorrows and joys that we do not feel in that moment. Christ, praying the

---

15. In *Spiritual Emotions: A Psychology of Christian Virtues* (Grand Rapids: Eerdmans, 2007), Robert C. Roberts describes emotions not as irrational eruptions but as "concern-based construals" (11). By this he means that emotional responses occur in relation to those things that we are concerned about: anger from something we love being disturbed, joy from something we value being presented to us, and so on. In this way, emotions follow from those things that we learn to care about and value rather than being indicators prima facie of what things are to be valued.

16. Dietrich Bonhoeffer, *Prayerbook of the Bible: An Introduction to the Psalms*, trans. James H. Burtness, in *Life Together; Prayerbook of the Bible*, Dietrich Bonhoeffer Works 5 (Minneapolis: Fortress, 1996), 156: "God's speech in Jesus Christ meets us in the Holy Scriptures. If we want to pray with assurance and joy, then the word of Holy Scripture must be the firm foundation of our prayer. Here we know that Jesus Christ, the Word of God, teaches us to pray." Augustine, in his exposition on Psalm 3, says much the same: "The psalm can be understood with reference to the person of Christ in another way, namely, that the whole Christ is speaking: Christ in his totality, I say, in concert with his body of which he is the Head" (*Exposition of the Psalms*, vol. 1, trans. Maria Boulding and Edmund Hill, The Works of Saint Augustine III/15 [New York: New City Press, 2000], 81).

Psalms, leads the congregation forward, together, to embrace a world that is alien to it in the moment.[17] Gathered up together, the congregation follows the lead of Christ in praying the Scriptures that it does not feel, led toward alien sentiments, trained together concerning the confessions it must make, though it may not yet know those thoughts as its own.[18] The Old Testament, as Christ's own Scriptures, and the New Testament, as authored by God's own people, come together in Christ's person. And so, our reading together of the Scriptures, as one body, is an invitation to be shaped together toward those things that we should love, the promises that we should believe, and the hope we should embody.

Though done in one location, this work joins one congregation to another. In Christ, our readings of the Scriptures, whether done together at the home table at the start of the day or at church to begin our worship, cease to be simply in-house readings, for we are reading in Christ, who joins the scattered body together. To say this differently, when done together, with Christ as the focus, our local readings of the Scriptures are invited to become catholic readings, shared readings of the people of God, regardless of the ecclesiological commitments to autonomy or diocesan authority that exist. What materially might happen through the use of common readings such as a Book of Common Prayer is formally possible only because we are joined into the person of Christ, who prays the promises and the ranges of experience of the Scriptures for us, because he is the vicarious human for all humanity.

The theology of our reading—that we are being shaped together and not solely according to our individual connections to this or that sentiment within Scripture—is continued by *how* we read together, when the reading of Scripture becomes a shared venture of all members, allowing children and adults, excellent readers and halting ones to take turns. This not only emphasizes how the Scriptures are the common Word of God for the people of God; it also refuses to

17. Bonhoeffer, *Life Together*, 55: "The Psalter is the vicarious prayer of Christ for his congregation. Now that Christ is with the Father, the new humanity of Christ—the body of Christ—on earth continues to pray his prayer to the end of time."

18. Bonhoeffer, *Life Together*, 57: "What happened to us on the cross of Christ, the death of our old self, . . . is what gives us the right to pray these prayers."

let the ability of some dominate the reading or performance of the Scriptures.[19] This is not to say that all interpretations of Scripture are created equal (which we will return to shortly) but rather that all *reading* of Scripture is done by members of the community *as* members: we are not the primary speaker or author of Scripture, and our feelings or experiences are not to be identified with Scripture itself. We always read as a member of a community, the young with the old, the excellent with the novice, bound up with other communities, with Christ as the one we hear together.

To read the Scriptures in this way, which refuses isolation from others in their performance, also reminds us that the moment in which we live is linked together with other moments and with a history that is our own true history: the history of Scripture. We are not the first people to suffer, nor are we the last, and thus our suffering is both novel and not; because of this, our suffering finds its meaning in the presence of Christ, who prays the words of Scripture with us. A perennial temptation here is to look to the Scriptures to find echoes of our own suffering, sadness, or joy, but this is, as we have seen, only the road back into isolation. It is not so much that God does not speak to the intimacies of the person, but when we are gathered together, this is not the primary focus. Scripture is not *my* history but rather a history I am joined to: we are branches grafted into a tree that has been growing for eons, and we find the meaning of our existence not in our impermeable selves but in the textured, generous history of the people of God over time.

But sheer *reading* must give way to *interpretation*. Here, let me say that, within a vision of the community joined together, it does not entail that all interpretations are created equally. What I mean is this: It does churches no favor to say that unity is equated with equal portions of wisdom, interpretive skill, or maturity. To say that we have a united community of readers and interpreters is not to say that all interpretation coheres either with the witness of Scripture itself or with the wisdom of Christian readings over time.

One possible solution here is to simply adopt a traditional Catholic approach, which emphasizes the priority of the ancient church's

19. Bonhoeffer, *Life Together*, 63–64.

teachings; while it is right to defer to the witness of those closest chronologically to Scripture, adopting this approach wholesale has the unintended tendency to stop conversation concerning how the Scriptures might be plausibly read in ways consonant with the past.[20] But Stephen Fowl and Greg Jones offer a different alternative. They propose that these difficulties of divergent readings are overcome not necessarily only by appeal to how ancient the interpretation is but by attention to the witness produced by the reading, by testing the character of the ones proposing the reading. For the good tree bears good fruit, no matter how young the tree or how alien to the church culture the tree might look.[21]

But this is only part of the solution here. For a reading of Scripture may very well be consistent with the fruits of the Spirit and yet still be insufficient: a virtuous reader may yet be ignorant, exhibiting the holiness of Christ but offering a reading that speaks strangely of the nature of God—for example, drawing a reading from Scripture that is alien to Christians historically considered. If the intent here is to read the Scriptures as a community while simultaneously acknowledging the unevenness of interpretation for the reasons named above, an alternative to suppression appears: curiosity. It may be that the reading offered from within is not so much errant as untested. To test whether this is the case, a congregation ought to do its interpretations with those outside it, those who offer strange fruit to the congregation but who likewise share "sufficient common ground"—that is, a common Scripture and a common God.[22] Rather than outright refusing the new reading on the grounds that it is new or on-the-face dissonant with received interpretation, the church proceeds from the assumption that the new reading that has emerged is alien and yet comes from one who is family, a member of the church-community.

In other words, by exercising patience in its hearing, the church not only gains facility in testing its reading of Scripture in consonance with

---

20. For this account, see Richard R. Gaillardetz, *By What Authority? A Primer on Scripture, Magisterium, and the Sense of the Faithful* (Collegeville, MN: Liturgical Press, 2003), particularly 74–89.

21. Stephen E. Fowl and L. Gregory Jones, *Reading in Communion* (Eugene, OR: Wipf & Stock, 1998), 78.

22. Fowl and Jones, *Reading in Communion*, 126–28.

the wider and yet alien body of Christ (both in the form of the received and historic traditions of the church, and with other congregations beyond their own) but also gains the eyes to see those *inside its body* whom it might be otherwise inclined to ignore. As we saw with respect to Matthew 25, the priority of the isolated prisoner with respect to understanding our spiritual condition is also the figure of how we proceed with interpretive disagreement: attending to the strange readings first, as possible gifts, and attending to the ones who bring those readings as strange gifts among us who we would otherwise be inclined to overlook.

The way in which these Scriptures are preached follows from this as well. The centrality of the preached Word, the proclaimed promises of God, too, turns us away from our own insights and invites us to have our wisdom, passions, and virtue shaped together by the common Scriptures proclaimed.[23] Preaching is not first an occasion to be clever but to draw out a picture of God's work across time. Preaching serves not to conform the hearer to the speaker but to invite to inquiry, to help the congregation find their questions' homes within the Scriptures: these questions are not the shape of the house, but any house must ultimately be lived in, with all the bumps, rearrangements, and rhythms of that life.[24] The search for what God says through Scripture to the congregation must be a shared venture for preacher and congregation, an invitation into shared submission, so that we might have a shared life under the Word. Far from an abandonment of discernment and wisdom, the shared Scriptures offer an opportunity for our shared world to be spoken to by Scripture, coaxing the way of discipleship into existence as the congregation listens together for God's Word and bears this out in the shape of its practice through questioning together and reasoning together about what has been proclaimed.[25]

23. On Bonhoeffer's own theology of preaching, see in particular Michael Pasquarello III, *Dietrich Bonhoeffer and the Theology of a Preaching Life* (Waco: Baylor University Press, 2017); and Frits de Lange, *Waiting for the Word: Dietrich Bonhoeffer on Speaking about God* (Grand Rapids: Eerdmans, 2000).

24. Dietrich Bonhoeffer, *Theological Education at Finkenwalde: 1935–1937*, trans. Douglas W. Stott, Dietrich Bonhoeffer Works 14 (Minneapolis: Fortress, 2013), 167: "One cannot simply read the Bible like other books; one must be prepared genuinely to query it."

25. The Scriptures, as God's contemporaneous word, were to be heard not as accommodations to our questions but as a refinement, valuing, and repositioning of

Joining the Song of Creation

If the redemption of creation—of time and of our isolated state—
begins with Scripture (in its reading, discussion, and preaching), it
continues in the form of our singing. If with the reading of Scripture
we are commended to join with the history of God's people, learning
how we are to be instead of fitting Scripture into our experience, so
the act of our *singing* continues this work. Consider here the songs
recorded in Scripture, whether the song of Hannah, the Psalms, the
Magnificat, the Christus hymn, or the songs of the angels in Revelation: these are songs that, above all, speak of God, emplotting
the singer into a history that precedes them. Whether we sing them
together, like the Psalms, or alone, like the Magnificat, we find not
songs that drive deeper into our own experience but singing that
draws us as singers together into our shared history with Scripture.[26]

In singing, the church is primarily oriented not toward giving voice
to one's own experience but toward joining with the praise of God
by the cosmos. The Psalms, born out of a community's pain, joy,
and struggle, are bracketed and made possible by a different kind of
song, the songs of the angels in Revelation and at the nativity, the
thunderous clamor of Job 38, the cries of rocks and clapping hands
of trees. Our songs are, in other words, participating in the broader
tapestry of created reality, making us—like the Psalms—eccentric,
drawn out of ourselves toward God.[27] Our singing as a participation
with entities that lie beyond both our control and our comparison—
with nature and with angels—links the work of the gathered body
of Christ into God's manifold work; the church's work is not for its
own betterment but for displaying this manifold joy in all dimensions
of reality. As the temporality of the church participates in its eternal
reality, so the songs of the church join it together in the music sung

---

our questions within the world of Scripture. See Pasquarello, *Dietrich Bonhoeffer
and the Theology of a Preaching Life*, 141–43.

26. Brian Brock, *Singing the Ethos of God: On the Place of Christian Ethics in
Scripture* (Grand Rapids: Eerdmans, 2007), 272–74, has made the case that before
ethics can be enacted, it must be sung in the church's worship, incorporating modes
of behaviors into our worship both as a testing point and as entering into the world
created by language.

27. Bonhoeffer, *Life Together*, 65.

by the saints; it is one way that the church militant and the church triumphant are of one piece, joined together in the flesh of Christ.

When we think about our singing as it relates to the question of isolation, then, placing one's own experience within a broader frame avoids one specter: that of the isolated individual. The songs of the community are not to be those that simply give voice to the inscrutable experience of the individual, emphasizing either felt piety or singular lament. These exchange the shared story of Scripture for the impenetrable depths of our own pain, ironically driving us deeper into our own feelings, which cannot be shared or known by others. But isolation's second face—the crowd—requires us to not hide collectively behind the Scriptures either in offering our praise or in refusing to offer our own voices. Even within the Scriptures, the hymns that we find embedded in the walls of Philippians, Colossians, and the Gospels are not mere repetitions of other Scripture passages: Scripture itself contains improvisations on itself, the words of Malachi and Isaiah and Genesis amplified and expanded as they enter new houses and mix with new words.[28]

In taking our cues from how the Scriptures bind us together in their common reading, we can assume a parameter: the songs of the community are meant to be amplifications and rehearsals of Scripture, not replacements for it. In this way, we join the singing of our house with the ongoing song of the people of God. The songs of the people are to be the songs *of the people* before God, both in form and substance: sung by the group and the gift of the group in the words and performance.

In their practice, then, songs reflect this not only in their substance (continuity with and expansion of Scripture, joining us together with the community of God) but also in the form of the singing. In a surprising set of remarks, Bonhoeffer calls for a style of singing unadorned by expertise or complexity, emphasizing the "purity

---

28. In his *Improvisation: The Drama of Christian Ethics* (Grand Rapids: Brazos, 2004), 59–70, Samuel Wells makes the case that the Scriptures constitute not a finished drama (contrary to the arguments of N. T. Wright) but an open-ended drama that invites improvisation in light of Scripture. Eschatologically, the story spoken of in Scripture is of a piece with our own world, such that God's people contain trajectories that Scripture outlines but cannot dictate the specific verbiage of.

of unison singing—untouched by the unrelated motives of musical excess."[29] This counsel runs against the grain of traditions of music in which the orchestration ornaments the text or in which the text provides a point of departure for the composition.[30] This way of thinking about the relationship between text and instrumentation—ornamentation and amplification of the text—runs two risks: not only is our attention drawn to the performance of the music (turning the congregation into a crowd gathered around a common experience), but this approach elevates the gifts of those so musically inclined over against the work of the whole community (amplifying the presupposition that our gifts are individually cultivated and appreciated).

In turning to a plainer style of singing, the community offers together one voice of their confession as opposed to letting one person (a soloist or a virtuoso, or more recently in vogue, the "lead worshiper") offer their interpretation as the word of the congregation. Calling forth the gifts of the congregation as a whole, by contrast, reinforces what our hymns and praises are—offerings that join us to the song of creation and acts concerned with mirroring God's intent for that creation (in this case, unity) by expressing that intent in ways that do not let aesthetics overdetermine the course of singing. Beauty, after all, is indexed to order, such that what is more beautiful in the congregation's singing is that it is done as a community, not that it is on pitch or that it is of orchestral quality.

Praying the Prayers of the Community

What we have been offering thus far is an account of the practices of the church as interconnected and mutually reinforcing, as the vision of Scripture and of our singing are oriented toward embodying the renewal of the world in Christ.[31] But no practice, perhaps, is more susceptible to decay here than prayer, if only because the

29. Bonhoeffer, *Life Together*, 67.

30. To the dismay of my Church of Christ colleagues, Bonhoeffer is not here offering a critique rooted in a desire for restoration of early church practice.

31. Bonhoeffer, *Life Together*, 61: "God's Word, the voice of the Church, and our prayers belong together."

object of our prayers—God—is not visible to us, and so our act of praying to the God unseen tempts us to forget the visible ones we pray among. Our prayers are rightly to be directed only to God, but it is God's people that we have been given to pray on behalf of, with, and for.

To begin, let us return to Bonhoeffer's commentary on Genesis, in which the serpent's words indicate how prayer as speech toward God goes wrong: "The conversation [between the serpent and the woman] continues—the first conversation *about* God, the first religious, theological conversation. It is not common worship, a common calling upon God, but a speaking about God, about God in a way that passes over, and reaches beyond, God."[32] The reference here to the first "religious, theological conversation" is not a positive one, for it references an objectifying of God rather than a worship of God. This is not to say that theological conversation is wrong—far from it! The implications here for theological education are far ranging, but it is in prayer that this critique is most acute.[33] In prayer, the point is not the dissection of God as an object but rather participation in the life of God as a member of Christ's body. When we approach corporate prayer in a way that not only judges the words offered in prayer but judges them according to the canons of wisdom of the *individual*, then not only do we break away from the community in prayer, but we place ourselves as the judge of the community *and* of the God who has called the pray-er into it.

This is not to say that there is no place for judgment of our language in the body of Christ; to speak of God faithfully is to speak of God carefully, and not in vain, to not endlessly babble like the pagans

32. Dietrich Bonhoeffer, *Creation and Fall: A Theological Exposition of Genesis 1–3*, trans. Douglas Stephen Bax, Dietrich Bonhoeffer Works 3 (Minneapolis: Fortress, 1997), 111–12.

33. For a compelling account of theological education as a theological (i.e., doxological) exercise, see Adam Neder, *Theology as a Way of Life: On Teaching and Learning the Christian Faith* (Grand Rapids: Baker Academic, 2019). Neder's account of theological education as a matter of becoming the reconciled creatures in Christ that we are (15) deserves wider attention, as it echoes many of the presuppositions of a more classic approach to Christian pedagogy, in which prayer and intellect were companions. See Anselm, *Proslogion*, in *Anselm of Canterbury: The Major Works* (Oxford: Oxford University Press, 2008), 82–105, for one formal example of this marriage of prayer and intellect.

or to pray as those without hope.[34] The corporate prayer is the occasion to offer one's prayers as they are prayed by another, to set aside aesthetic judgments and offer one's prayers in humility as they are led by the words of another. Having heard the promises of Scripture together, we then offer our voices together in song and in prayer, but in a way that adds *our* words to those words that have come before us. Our prayer, like our song and our reflection on Scripture, enters into the stream of what has come before us, but it is not concerned with simply repeating the words of the past as if these were the only words that could be spoken or as if the present were not a moment of God's concern. Individual pains, variegated sufferings, and struggles unique to a particular family are of concern to God and are not to be forgotten: the community is not a crowd in which persons are interchangeable parts. Therefore, the prayers, petitions, and gratitude voiced by a particular congregation add to the prayers of the church across time—they are the gifts that could only ever be given by *this* congregation in *this* place!

As we emphasize the *corporate* prayers of the people first, individual pray-ers find not only their context but also their freedom to pray with the heart of the community. When we are alone, others remain unknown to us, and in a crowd we are not joining our concerns together, but in a community the common voice of prayer lays the ground for our improvisations on the theme. Our prayers as individuals begin by first interceding for others, for this is the economy by which we as individuals even come to pray in the first place. If prayer does not bring us deeper into this common work of God but splits us from it, we are giving in to the first temptation, for we are placing ourselves not only over against the work of God but over against God's wisdom of having this body in the first place.[35]

We are pray-ers because we have been taught to pray, nurtured among other pray-ers, and we are pray-ers not so we can pray for

---

34. See on this point *Catechism of the Catholic Church* (New York: Doubleday, 1995), 577–78, on taking the Lord's name in vain.

35. Bonhoeffer, *Life Together*, 69: "How could one person pray the prayer of the fellowship without being steadied and upheld in prayer by the fellowship itself? At precisely this point every word of criticism must be transformed into more faithful intercession and mutual help."

ourselves but so we can pray with others. Recall the number of times, for example, both in the Psalms and in the letters of the New Testament, that the prayers—offered by individual authors—are inextricable from the concerns and future of the community. It is not that we should not pray for our own concerns but that we should remember that we pray as a member of a body, inextricable from its pain and its redemption. In the same way that our concerns and content of prayer join us to the body of Christ, the *form* of our prayers does as well. As with Scripture and song, our prayers are meant to join us to this new world that Christ has called into being, to participate in the redemption of creation—of time and of our isolated state. In the same way, prayer should follow the rhythms of the day—morning and evening, organized by monotony, freely embracing the mundane rhythms of a day: in this way, in the repetitions of praying for the same things day after day with the church, our prayers are freedom from the starting point of our own introspective needs.[36]

There is a freedom from the burdens of our own selves here in prayer, for the subject of prayer is not that which has to be dredged up from memory each week; rather, the subjects of prayer are those that are presented to us regularly from the outside, both from the concerns of Scripture and from the life of the church that we are committed to. We need not think up things to pray for, for when our individual prayers follow from our common life, and we thus pray for those whom we know in worship, we are regularly joined to the body of Christ and their concerns.

This form of prayer likewise frees us from prayer being a matter of individual motivation, for morning comes every day along with the evening, whether we feel like it or not: prescribed prayer allows not only our theology, our practice, and our vision of time but also our sense of desire for prayer to be re-created. Desire is not a value-neutral aspect of our constitution as humans, but that which is cultivated according to the objects presented to it: in having our prayer guided, we learn *how* and *what* to love rather than assuming that our intuitive loves are sufficient. Therefore, we begin to desire the subject of

36. Bonhoeffer, *Life Together*, 70. More will be said in the following chapter on individual introspection and prayer.

prayer not by searching it out from the recesses of memory but by having its objects regularly presented to us.

No longer captive by our own motivation in prayer or perfection of form or depth of feeling, we are freed in the end to pray in our own words, knowing that their particularity—not their perfection—matters as a part of the body. We can pray our specific prayers and concerns, for we know that prayer is neither begun by us (but by the Spirit within us) nor determined by our affective state (but by the rhythms of creation and Scripture), and the God who has joined me to the body has joined *me* to the body. By praying as those who are enlivened by the Spirit and joined to the body of Christ, we can offer our own words, our own prayers, freely, for there is none who prays except through Christ's work, the Christ who joins us in our prayers for one another and creation.

Eating the Common Bread

In each of the previous practices, what the church does in its day together finds interrelation with smaller groups: what we do in church is mirrored at home and other small groups, whether named "discipleship groups," "cell groups," "community groups," or the like. Acknowledging the validity and goodness of these, though, is not a call for us to reinvent the wheel in each new context, for what we do apart from the church is theologically framed by the center of creation: God's work in Christ, seen in Christ's body of the church. The ways in which we pray together as families, or as roommates, or with our weekly community groups are framed by our common prayers in the church. Likewise, the ways in which we eat together find their center in the meal of the church: the table of Communion.

In my own Baptist tradition, the memorialist approach—doing the meal in reverential memory of Christ's work—is prominent, emphasizing the ways in which the work of Christ is present to our memory. The participant recalls the work of Christ, mediated through our own experiences and testimony, recalling the ways in which God has worked out salvation in the deep seams of our life. As opposed to traditions that emphasize the presence of Christ in cup and bread, the memorialist approach—one more widely adopted by any number of "low church" groups—approaches the meal in a symbolic fashion, not to minimize its importance but to emphasize the *promeity* (the "for our benefit-ness") of the meal: Christ's work is linked to what Christ has done in my own life. In the memorialist understanding, we remember Christ's work and efficacious power in tandem with the specifics of how Christ has changed our particular lives.

The danger this approach runs, however, is mediating the meaning of Communion *first* by the contours of memory, such that any further meaning of Communion becomes an extension of my own testimony. As with personal prayers or personal readings of Scripture, the problem is not that these improvisations exist but that these remembrances and meditations frequently displace the common work of Christ and simply repeat the errors of isolation. It is not enough here to say, with Stanley Grenz, that because these acts are done together we are on our way beyond memorialism, for even in a crowd, these remain isolated acts.[37] What we have in the bread and wine is not of our own making but is the common gift of God to the church, to be received in a way that incorporates us into the common gift, so that we might add the flourishes of Christ's work in this place and in that place to that common center.[38]

Each table—first in the church's gathering, then in all other gatherings, whether with roommates or family, in nursing homes or in prison fellowships—is a real place of fellowship, though real insofar as it is a signpost of the kingdom of God. And as such, these tables guide us and reinforce in us our belonging in the body of Christ, reminding us not of ourselves and our love for one another but of the one body of Christ of which all Christians partake. As a Lutheran, Bonhoeffer places great weight on the presence of Christ in the act of Communion, but if these *other* tables are divided from the Communion table, we have missed the point: Christ desires to reunite the

---

37. Stanley Grenz, "Baptism and the Lord's Supper as Community Acts: Toward a Sacramental Understanding of the Ordinances," in *Baptist Sacramentalism*, ed. Anthony R. Cross and Philip E. Thompson (Eugene, OR: Wipf & Stock, 2003), 76–95.

38. Miroslav Volf, "Memory, Eschatology, Eucharist," *Liturgy* 1 (2007): 27–38, links memory of Christ's crucifixion to the dynamics of our own remembering of past wrongs done to us, drawing together the atoning work of Christ and the way in which we misremember our social lives with others.

whole of creation, such that what occurs in the body of Christ echoes outward throughout all creation. There is no either/or of church or world, of locating Christ's work in either the world or the church, for isolation and fragmentation, as we have seen, are not a problem of society alone but are often replicated unwittingly by the church. Likewise, the fragmenting of creation into discrete and divided segments of home, work, and church assumes an insularity to a context such that Christ's presence can appear only in a kind of altered form.

Because Christ is present truly in our gathered meals as the church, we can affirm Christ's true presence, by analogy, in all of our gatherings.[39] In the First Letter to the Corinthians, there is a reason that Paul speaks so strongly about how the Corinthians eat together: their moral abuses of one another and the disrespect they show to the table are of one piece. When they eat together in a way that prioritizes the rich over the poor, it is because they disrespect the presence of Christ among them as the body. When we engage in gluttony, we are dishonoring the ubiquitous nature of God's gift; when we eat inhospitably, we create divisions among the body in the name of protecting and fencing the table.[40] This is not to wade into the questions of *how* Christ is present among participants (questions that Luther and Bonhoeffer found to be the wrong questions)[41] but rather to affirm

39. Bonhoeffer, *Life Together*, 73: "*Every* breaking of bread together fills Christians with gratitude for the present Lord and God, Jesus Christ" (emphasis added).

40. The Reformation arguments over the "fencing of the table" were not made to withhold the meal but to protect those who would eat it in an unworthy fashion. For a detailed engagement with these historic differences, see George Hunsinger, *The Eucharist and Ecumenism: Let Us Keep the Feast* (Cambridge: Cambridge University Press, 2008). Hunsinger, at the outset, sets aside memorialist traditions in his work, which likewise means that these traditions are not included in ecumenical work. While I agree with Hunsinger that memorialism needs renovation, the solution is not to exclude these memorialist groups who nonetheless practice Communion from ecumenical conversations but to ask in what ways Christ is understood to be likewise present in these groups, unless one does not think them to in fact be members of the universal body of Christ.

41. For Luther's best-known articulation of his objections to arguments surrounding transubstantiation, see *The Pagan Servitude of the Church* (1520), in *Martin Luther: Selections from His Writings*, ed. John Dillenberger (New York: Doubleday, 1961), 249–362. For Bonhoeffer, see his comments in his lectures on Christology, in which he emphasizes not the "how" but the "what" of God's presence to us in Christ: "Lectures on Christology," in Dietrich Bonhoeffer, *Berlin: 1932–1933*,

that Christ's very presence *is* among us when we eat. For the meals that we share—as the church or at home—are common meals: we are bound to one another in these events because of our share in Christ together, and our meals signify this seriousness whenever they occur.

Eating together is, by its nature, the fulfilling of one person's need by the act of another, a natural analogy to the act of Communion.[42] To partake of any meal is already to partake of a shared gift of creation, for the rain falls on the just and unjust. And to partake of any meal is to partake of the gratuity of God toward the world, a gratuity that we share with the neighbors we know and with our enemies. And so, the very act of eating—specified in our shared meal together as the church and echoed elsewhere—is a shared and unifying act by its nature, and it is in the act of Communion that we see the heart of eating everywhere. In Communion, we share of God's graciousness, a graciousness shared with the friend and the enemy, the sinner and the saint. By it, we see that the act of eating together, likewise, is a time of formation: in eating, we draw from outside ourselves what we need to live, from the hands of another, to strengthen us in the life that proceeds only from God. In our practices of eating, then, we can view these as sheer transactions or as opportunities for gratitude and exchange. Our invitations to others to eat can be, as Jesus warned us (Luke 14:7–31), an opportunity to gain favor or an opportunity to extend a bridge to strangers, to nonfamiliars and to the isolated, a bridge that has been extended to us.

Witness and Mission in the Common World

The rhythm of our common life is not only one of prayer and worship but also one of shared labor and action. Communities, bodies in which the will is exercised toward one another, are not simply groups of idea exchange but of shared action. Communities differ

---

trans. Isabel Best and David Higgins, Dietrich Bonhoeffer Works 12 (Minneapolis: Fortress, 2009), 299–360.

42. It is with no small irony that the Baptist practice of potluck—a meal in which different aspects of the meal are provided by different members of the congregation—embodies this logic, despite Baptists' typically nonsacramental approach to Communion.

in this respect from other alternatives in that members carry out the mission not *alongside* one another (the crowd) or separately (the individual) but with one another. The "with"-ness of the labor and mission matters, for workers in a community do not merely divide the work up; rather, they labor in such a way that what each one does inflects how all the other parts function.

In Philippians, for example, we find Paul describing his own suffering and colaboring with the church, a church that has sent him not only money but Epaphroditus as well. In joining in the common mission of Paul in this way, the church in Philippi has had its affect altered: it suffers together with Paul, sharing his shame and aiding materially in his mission. This colaboring that becomes shared to the point of cosuffering indicates the life of the community, joined together in Christ in such a way that their labors and affections for the labors of another are interjoined.[43]

Like the prior practices, this too is a matter not only of drawing together the church into a body of communion but of renewing creation. The day together starts in prayer, but without common labor and mission the picture of our life together is incomplete.[44] Though most commonly found in monastic communities, this insight of work as inseparable from prayer is nothing new. In monastic communities of all stripes, prayer is accompanied by the practical tasks of running a community; in the Rule of Benedict, for example, the praying of the hours is punctuated by times of labor that are extensions of the life of worship.

It seems counterintuitive to say "labor" with respect to the gathered church, particularly when the days of our gathering are on the very day when we are called to *rest*: the Sabbath. The Sabbath is a day set aside for rest, but it is not as if the Sabbath were a day meant to be enjoyed away from the demands of others.[45] The Sabbath is not

43. See my essay "The Fellowship of Suffering: Reading Philippians 3:10 with Stanley Hauerwas," *Review and Expositor* 112 (2015): 144–50, on this point.

44. Bonhoeffer, *Life Together*, 75: "Without the burden and labor of the day, prayer is not prayer; and without prayer, work is not work."

45. Walter Brueggemann's *Sabbath as Resistance: Saying No to the Culture of Now* (Louisville: Westminster John Knox, 2017), 50–57, describes the ways in which the Sabbath is reflected on in the Hebrew Bible as a self-critical day of testing in which we are invited to consider whom we have made labor that we might be free of

a day free from the demands or the presence of others but rather a day when we return to restore that presence as an enduring feature of our communion with God. As Jesus teaches, the Sabbath, a day of worship, is also a day for feeding and restoring the body (Matt. 12:1–13) and loving the neighbor (Luke 14:1–6): acts intrinsic to the cultivation of our bodily communion with God.

Described in most Protestant circles as "mission," this labor goes by a different name in Catholic tradition: works of mercy.[46] The works of mercy, composed of both bodily and spiritual works, are not extraordinary actions, performed by extraordinary saints. Including such actions as attending and visiting the sick, clothing the naked, and instructing the ignorant, the life of mercy is already envisioned as that which extends outward from the table fellowship, materially extending the grace of Christ into the manifold fissures of the world.

In the act of common mission, prayer is extended and enacted, for it is in work that we add our flesh to the words of our prayers. In this, we are plunged into a very different world than the intimate and interpersonal world of prayer or of the table; it is uncontroversial to say that the world of mission is one that does not conform to our desires; or, to use the biblical metaphor, grow crops where and when we sow. All the more reason, then, for us to include this dimension to be aware of both how we are *rightly* formed in common activity and how the arena of mission/works of mercy can be enacted in a way consistent with the vision of life together.

This dimension is important here precisely because it is *not* the same as prayer, for in working, we seek first to be disabused of the squishiness that often accompanies many community situations. In activities of mission (however conceived), we encounter the limit of our own ability to accomplish, the limit of another object that is impervious to my feelings: a task, a suspicious recipient for our

---

labor. This resonates with Abraham Joshua Heschel's account in *The Sabbath* (New York: Farrar, Straus & Giroux, 2005), 97–99, in which he writes that the Sabbath—in being a permeation of the eternal into time—occasions a criticism of our notions of owning time and space.

46. The introduction by James Keenan, SJ, *The Works of Mercy: The Heart of Catholicism* (New York: Rowman & Littlefield, 2017), describes the ordinary forms of these works.

gifts, a lawn to be mowed, an unyielding institutional process.[47] In encountering these tasks, our ego finds a limit to its ability to change the world, calling excellence and commitment out of us nonetheless. We commit ourselves to something that is not ours alone and to a task that is not an extension of our own will: we learn to give ourselves to a thing that is not us.

In working the world in mission, we can take the wrong lessons away and learn to instrumentalize the world and other people, treating these actions as acts to be accomplished rather than as acts by which we are being shaped: the lessons learned in recent years about the dangers of short-term missions are to be taken seriously here.[48] But there is another possibility—one that we carry into work if we look to mission to extend the work begun in prayer: that in work, we learn to be humble in our ego, to be committed to a task that is not immediately rewarded, and to give ourselves to what is not persuaded by our charm or charisma. Finding that limit is good, for in this limit we see that the same God who calls us to community is the God who trains us *for* that community, learning the limits of another person as we learn the limits found in the labor of missions.

We should envision the work of missions, in other words, *not* as an opportunity for us to impose our vision on the world but to bring the goods of the church into creation, acknowledging that our bringing the act of mission will also cultivate a real capacity for limits. In learning the limits that come with the act of mission, we continue the work of worship: to receive that gift of limits and dependence (on God, for our lives and for our communion with one another),

47. Bonhoeffer, *Life Together*, 75: "Christians learn at work to allow the task to set the bounds for them. Thus, for them, work becomes a remedy for the lethargy and laziness of the flesh."

48. The value of short-term missions for the participants, while transformative, also tends to reinforce the instrumentalization of missions toward the cultivation of individual virtues, not to attend primarily to the dynamics here—viewing mission as invitation, cultivation, and communion with the world beyond the church. See Terence Linhart, "They Were So Alive! The Spectacle Self and Youth Group Short-Term Mission Trips," *Missiology* 34 (2006): 451–62. An analogue for short-term missions, "voluntourism"—travel calibrated toward volunteer work—likewise falls prey to the same criticisms: travel calibrated less toward communion with those worked for and among, and more for the cultivation of the traveler's spiritual life.

that we might offer that gift back to the world in a way that images that gift as well.[49]

Without learning limits in this way, community life is not possible. Like the act of mission, a community is not an immediate benefit but a slow world grown out of commitment, trust, patience, and perseverance: it is not a formless void to be managed into existence but a gift of God to be tarried with because we do not know yet what form it will take. It is not without reason, then, that early Christian traditions—from the Apostolic Tradition to the Didache to the Liturgy of Hippolytus—all emphasize the ways in which our labors of the body constitute gifts brought to God, gifts that are meant to bless humanity in the doing.[50] This is, in a way, how the "work" of our gathered life—that is, the mission married to our worship—is married to the "work" we do on behalf of the world in Christ. It is important to note that the emphasis here is not on a certain kind of mission (evangelistic, service, or intellectual), nor is it even on productivity or success, but on offering our work of mission to the world in a form consistent with what is cultivated in our worship, and that which addresses itself to the needs in front of us.[51]

49. We will discuss the form of missions that befits this vision more fully within chapter 6.

50. See Matthew Kaemingk and Cory B. Wilson, *Work and Worship: Reconnecting Our Labor and Liturgy* (Grand Rapids: Baker Academic, 2020), 172–83.

51. That we make this assumption of mission is, I think, linked in no small part to the assumptions cultivated throughout the week: giving ourselves to a task that is not prayer encompasses the majority of days. And, though much of this goes uncompensated, all of this is what is meant as "work": the raising of children, the labor of the market, the tending of the household, the looking after of friends. It is an artificial and unjust arrangement by which we treat only those kinds of work that are *paid* as "work," and it is not the giving and receiving of money that makes work spiritually formative. As Virginia Held, *The Ethics of Care: Personal, Political, Global* (Oxford: Oxford University Press, 2007), 29–43, argues, the equation of "care" with "affection" distorts our vision of the ways in which certain forms of agency are compensated, and thus socially valued, while others are not. This elision proceeds along largely gendered assumptions of women as more inclined to affection than men. This creates in turn a division between public/work and private/home that continually prioritizes the political and public voices of men. The significance of this for our discussion is that, in the same way that we designate some acts as "work" and some as home necessities (valued in different ways), so we measure what counts as "mission" by the metric of what is most effective in terms of amplifying the mission, message, or numerical value of the church. As we shall see, this is detrimental to an

The vision, instituted here as the church, likewise shapes our common, gathered life at other tables and in other houses. One way is the more idyllic form of work advocated for by those such as Wendell Berry: shifting the locus of work to the home, such that there is not a hard divide between the life of labor and the life of family.[52] And though Berry means something more radical than a makeshift and temporary arrangement, his basic premise of knitting back together the world of work and the world of home is similar to what is meant here: the world of work is to be conducted as a matter of "making space" for Christ, of reintegrating a world that has been fractured. Prayer and devotion are not simply a matter of what one does at home but are the *shape* of how the life of work occurs.

The Theologic of Our Day Together: Union of the Weak and Strong

The proposals on offer—whether congregational singing instead of ornamented singing, our common mission, or common reading—rely on an important presupposition of community, as opposed to the crowd: the union of the weak and the strong. In Paul's descriptions of the gifts of the body, he repeatedly exalts the gifts of "lesser value"— namely, those that do not attract attention or receive acclaim;[53] those gifts that are not viewed as the most aesthetically pleasing should likewise be brought together with those that are, so that all might join in the community of the church, as members of a common body. At stake here is the recognition that the church-community is composed not of members who are the same but of members whose gifts and status create an unevenness of the "weak" and "strong," whether in

---

understanding of community, for it "devalues" the gifts and agency of some as not "contributing" to the church.

52. Berry writes of this proposal in multiple places, most concisely in *Sex, Economy, Freedom & Community: Eight Essays* (New York: Pantheon Books, 1993).

53. 1 Corinthians 12:22–25: "On the contrary, the members of the body that seem to be weaker are indispensable, and those members of the body that we think less honorable we clothe with greater honor, and our less respectable members are treated with greater respect; whereas our more respectable members do not need this. But God has so arranged the body, giving the greater honor to the inferior member, that there may be no dissension within the body, but the members may have the same care for one another."

terms of spiritual maturity, divergences of life experience, or differences of race, gender, or age. And no amount of common singing or
sharing of Scripture reading can efface that.[54]

These differences, and the disparities that are attributed to these
differences by society, are to be seen soberly; we must not impose
some kind of false similarity over the whole congregation: saying
that we are "one in Christ" does not mean flattening distinctions or
overlooking disparities or assuming a common maturity among all
members of the congregation, whether with respect to evaluating
singing abilities or evaluating doctrinal coherence.[55] If the logic of the
individual is to exalt the most talented, it is the logic of the crowd to
impose a superficial democratic sameness on abilities and gifts. Being
part of a community, composed of persons joined together into a
single body, means taking seriously these differences and disparities,
ordering our relations, gifts, and talents toward others rather than letting a pursuit of unity cause differences—whether those (positively)
of gifting, life experience, or maturity or (negatively) those created
by injustice and prejudices—to remain unseen and unable to offer
their gifts (positively) or be redressed (negatively).

As seen already, in our singing it would mean using those gifts to
cultivate the singing of others; in reading Scripture, giving opportunity for the young, the overlooked, and the halting of speech to
be readers as well as the sonorous; in our interpreting of Scripture,
exercising critical charity toward readings coming out of divergent
life experience and politics; or in our missions, praising the young and
the ones working behind the scenes. But within all areas, addressing
church unity by assuming a uniformity of experience, gifting, or lack
of obstacles is to ignore the actual bodies of the body of Christ before
us: by not seeing bodies and their particularities, we do not see the

---

54. In naming "weak" and "strong," I am following Bonhoeffer's expansion of
the term in reference to difference within a community that is not always indexed to
capacity but to perceived inequality of capacity: not all "weaknesses" are objectively
such, though they may, within the framework from which the church emerges, be
perceived as such.

55. On this point, the language of "reconciliation" has rightly been criticized for
moving too quickly past difference and historic wrongs to emphasize reunion. See in
particular Jennifer Harvey, *Dear White Christians: For Those Still Longing for Racial
Reconciliation* (Grand Rapids: Eerdmans, 2020), 63–94.

contour of the body of Christ and the works of reconciliation that Christ is doing among us.

The purpose in emphasizing the distinctions rather than commonalities is not to produce again a church rooted in endless differentiation but to confess that we do not yet know the new shape that our communion will entail. Once the differences are named, difference becomes either (1) the new point of commonality (i.e., that we are all unique) or (2) the new aggregation machine binding subsections of a congregation. But difference requires recognition to be realized—a difference that *makes* no difference is simply an aesthetic. By acknowledging and inquiring with curiosity into the differences within a commonly shared habit—of singing, eating, reading, and serving—we allow the differences to remain and we are invited to let those differences be an occasion for curiosity. The differences can be an occasion to isolate or an invitation for me to ask, *What is it about this strangeness that I do not understand? What does this strangeness ask me to receive? And what must I let go of in order to receive this gift?*

Does this emphasis on the congregation together—in its reading and singing—flatten not only the wisdom of some readers of Scripture but also the difference of gifts that make up the church? If someone has aptitude in reading and interpreting Scripture or has giftedness in leading song, should their gifts be submerged? What is important here is not that those who are gifted in these areas hide their gifts but that they use their gifts to cultivate the capacities of the church as a whole. If the aim here is not only to facilitate the church's corporate life but to administer a therapy for our isolation, then it is not so much that extraordinary musical gifts, divergent life stories, or disproportionate experiences of injustice are seen as non-gifts. It is rather that these gifts must serve the "weaker" members of the group, lifting them up instead of worshiping on their behalf, ministering in their name, or speaking as their proxy.

The Life Together: Beginning to End

Isolation haunts all of our life together—indeed, it is woven into the very conditions that in many ways make our world. The proliferation of denigrating forms of free enterprise, of sports, of our educational systems—all of which foster individual initiative and competition—are contingent on viewing the world as being the struggle of individuals all the way down. Retraining this sensibility and learning a different world—the one brought into being in and through Christ—requires nothing less than ordering the day together from beginning to end in its light.

But the critical component is that our life together is that which we must be habituated into and that our life together is how the Scriptures "work": we are invited to live into the world of Scripture, to locate our world within the world of Scripture. We learn this new world of Scripture slowly, letting its vision of God's communal work judge, reshape, and reorder the mundane and profound elements of our worship. The implications for the gathered life of church communities are manifold, for this vision challenges our habits of Scripture reading and interpretation, our choices as to whom we work and eat alongside and whom we take our cues from within the church fellowship, and our understanding of what our giftedness is for.

But to simply call for a renewal of our gathered and common life is not enough for exploring how isolation is undone. As we have argued already, isolation comes with being a creature in the creation after the fall, and as such the theological therapy must continue by examining how we live apart from the gathered church. The challenge here is to conceive of this life apart from the gathered church not as some other existence, something we do as a concession or a secondary form of existence, but as an extension of the community of the church. It is to this we now turn.

Five

Restructuring Private Life

Practicing Christian community could not possibly mean that all one does is gather together, never separating out from others. To only ever think about the nature of the church-community when we are gathered is to occlude the fact that much of our lives are lived apart from one another. In many *ressourcements* of Christian community, the formations of liturgy are overplayed in this way: though the life of community shapes us in important ways, we carry all of what we are into the community, formed already by alien liturgies and practices.

Attention to the ways in which we are apart and to their relation to our life together is important not only for practical reasons but also for theological reasons; without a renewal of the depths of what a person is, apart from their gathering, the crux of isolation remains—we return to the gathered body to avoid having to answer the ongoing question, Who am I? In a crowd, questions and provocations of this kind can be deferred. Apart from attending to the times in which we are apart—whether through work, leisure, or unintentional times of separation—we will only ever look to groups as a place to hide, a place to escape, a respite from being alone. For a true *community* to emerge, it must be composed of those who are being freed from the need to hide, from God and from others.

The "day apart" is what Bonhoeffer calls these days, those myriad spaces between our corporate gatherings, the necessary counterpoint to life in community. Rather than thinking of these times in terms of absence between gatherings, consider this analogy: times apart are to our gathered lives as periods, commas, and spaces between words are to the structure of sentences. Without them, the specific words lose shape, for the breaths between words are as much a part of our speech as the consonants and vowels. The refraining from speech remains part of the act of speech. Likewise, our time apart belongs to the structure of our gathering, knit within the overarching concern for forming a people of God out of aggregated fragments.

The Day Apart: *Askesis* and Mission

In Scripture, we find that we are not given into the world as individuals, and then as members of communities. We are first given to be with one another, from the birth of a child into a family they did not choose to our incorporation into Christ's body, alongside members I did not call or sanctify. In the same way, our identity when we are scattered from the church is no less contingent on that community because of its absence: our gathered life shifts our concerns, our habits, and our points of reference, even when our fellow members are gone from us. For this change to take root—*from* the group-isolation and selfishness that a world in sin bears out, justifies, and institutionalizes *to* community—we must bear the tension of being called out from the community. But in this departure (to the ordinary rhythms of the week or perhaps to some more dramatic separation), we are engaging in a pedagogy not of isolation but of *solitude*. This counterpoint, the day apart, is indispensable for cultivating a life of community that is something other than alleviating the phenomenon of loneliness.[1]

If isolation is the condition of being divided from others—as a state and sometimes as a physical posture—solitude (being alone but

1. Dietrich Bonhoeffer, *Life Together*, trans. Daniel W. Bloesch, in *Life Together; Prayerbook of the Bible*, Dietrich Bonhoeffer Works 5 (Minneapolis: Fortress, 1996), 81: "Many persons seek community because they are afraid of loneliness. Because they can no longer endure being alone, such people are driven to seek the company of others."

oriented toward the community) is what best characterizes the "day apart." In solitude, as when we are with others, we will constantly be beset by temptations to hide from the state of isolation. Whereas in the day together, this takes the form of concealing our thinking from others, exhibiting false humility about our gifts, withholding our differences or weakness, in the "day apart" we are tempted by isolation by thinking of the world as divided spheres: church practice versus the necessities of the working world, the ideal of church contrasted to the realities of the world. But these divisions are false ones for a Christ in whom all things hang together, a Christ who stands at the center of reality.[2] The discipline of the day apart, then, involves unlearning our tendencies to separate church practice from individual practice, to normalize isolation in our lives beyond the gathered church.

That the church is embedded and entangled with the world is both a gift of God's grace, binding the church to its neighbors, and, as such, also a summons of the church to mission, bringing all those spaces in which our lives are formed when we are apart from the church-community together with that which is of the church. In what follows, we will describe the pedagogy of this "day apart": the pedagogy of solitude, which entails four different dimensions, all involved with rightly learning to value the community that is the body of Christ and extending the reach of the gathered body as it is scattered into the world.

The day alone exists alongside the day with the community, not only so that we might go through the *askesis* (practices of self-discipline) necessary to live in the community but also in order that

2. Bonhoeffer was keenly aware of the ways in which making some reserved space for God and apologetics that relied on God being the explanatory function of existence were part of the same logic: "It always seems to me that we are trying anxiously . . . to reserve some space for God; I should like to speak of God not on the boundaries but at the center, not in weakness but in strength; and therefore not in death and guilt but in man's life and goodness. . . . Belief in the resurrection is not the 'solution' of the problem of death. God's 'beyond' is not the beyond of our cognitive faculties. . . . God is beyond in the midst of our life. The church stands, not at the boundaries where human powers give out, but in the middle of the village" (Dietrich Bonhoeffer, *Letters and Papers from Prison*, trans. Isabel Best, Lisa E. Dahill, Reinhard Krauss, and Nancy Lukens, Dietrich Bonhoeffer Works 8 [Minneapolis: Fortress, 2010], 407–8).

we might know that the church-community exists both because God has called the church *and* because the God who loves the church also loves the world and desires it all to be God's kingdom. Without question, the church—the gathered people throughout creation—is Christ's body, the body that is given life by its head, exists spread out across time, and thus continues to live with sin.[3] So the reason we come out of the isolation of the world and gather in community is not to escape the isolation of sin—as if that were possible—for sin remains an ever-present possibility during time.

As we saw in the previous chapters, we do not escape the isolation of sin even while we are gathered; our time apart from the community is not thus the time we owe to isolation, paying back the world for the time we spend as the church. Rather, we are able to journey into creation *because we have been sent as emissaries of the community.* For the body of Christ is the ongoing minister of Christ's reconciliation, which means that it cannot exist solely as a gathered body apart from creation; it must also go out into creation that all might come in. It is, in other words, a body of mission that mirrors the sending of the Son into the world. We will bring any number of elements of these days back into our gathered life with us, not only so that the church might hear a witness that it might wish to ignore but also in order that the fractures of the world might be mended as they are brought in.

Embracing the Day Apart: Taking the Community with Us

In her book *Liturgy of the Ordinary,* Tish Harrison Warren offers a beautiful meditation on the ways in which ordinary practices become

3. Herbert McCabe puts it this way in *God Matters* (London: Continuum, 2005), 48: "The story of Jesus—which in its full extent is the entire Bible—is the projection of the trinitarian life of God on the rubbish dump that we have made of the world. The historical mission of Jesus is nothing other than the eternal mission of the Son from the Father; the historical outpouring of the Spirit in virtue of the passion, death and ascension is nothing but the eternal outpouring of the Spirit from the Father through the Son. Watching, so to say, the story of Jesus, we are watching the procession of the Trinity." The significance of this is the reminder that the intimate moments of the day apart are caught up within the singular and ongoing work of the triune God, who gathers the body to worship.

occasions for prayer. Whether making the bed, checking email, or sitting in traffic, we are invited to reflect on the truths of our gathered worship: the formative power of liturgy, the act of blessing with our words, the patient work of God. Her work in particular is an antidote to a separatist vision of church-community, a vision according to which it exists only when we are gathered, consigning us to isolation again in the intervening spaces.[4]

Warren helps us see one of the more straightforward temptations for the day apart and how to redress it. When we are in church it is easy to answer the question of the serpent—"Did God say that?"—with "Thus saith the Lord." But when we leave church and the question "Did God say that?" arises, we respond with simply, "God didn't say *that*"—that the Scriptures do not speak to the world of gas prices or nap times or market economies. The church is the church, and when scattered, we have to make the best of things, the argument goes.

By connecting regular rhythms of living to the life of the church, we are reminded that our lives as Christ's body are not governed solely by *principles* but by *practices* brought into the public square, that the habits we learn as church might shape our lives in all their mundane corners.[5] It is in this moment that we are tempted, having left church, to take up residence in the world in which we work, to raise children and pay taxes as if the Word of the Lord is not at home here. But it is only in having been in fellowship that we learn that when we are scattered out into the world, we are not scattered except as a moment set between gatherings: we are always already on our way back.

In departing, we learn that we can only be sustained apart from the body *by the body*: we can only maintain the Christian life as we

4. Tish Harrison Warren, *Liturgy of the Ordinary: Sacred Practices in Everyday Life* (Downers Grove, IL: InterVarsity, 2019).

5. Stanley Hauerwas, *The Peaceable Kingdom* (Notre Dame, IN: University of Notre Dame Press, 1983), 11. In making the claim for *practices* here instead of principles, I am not arguing for a pragmatist approach. I am instead arguing that our habits are born out in practices, in which wisdom is exercised as we live toward a telos. Our habits are manifested through the practices we exercise, and the practices are strengthened as the underlying habits governing them move from being simple dispositions (i.e., actions we might occasionally do) to habits (i.e., dispositions that become second nature to our thinking and behaving). Principles govern the kinds of habits we seek to have, but they are also affected, challenged, and nuanced by our habits.

recall to mind its goods and disciplines and take it into the world with us. And it is only by departing from the gathered body that we understand that it is not the gathered body *in and of itself* that saves us, but Christ, the one who gives life to the body. And it is this same Christ who sends out the seventy-two to do mundane things like speak, eat, walk, befriend, and in other ways serve as heralds of the coming kingdom.

In a later essay from Bonhoeffer's *Ethics* titled "Heritage and Decay," we see part of what is at stake when the day apart is conceived of as divided from our gathered life. The Reformation's emphasis on the freedom of the believer had become corrupted: "The original Reformation message, that human holiness is found neither in the sacred nor in the profane as such, but only through the gracious, sin-forgiving word of God, was thoroughly forgotten. The Reformation was celebrated as the liberation of the human being, of conscience, reason, and culture, as the justification of the worldly as such. . . . Its free use created an atmosphere of truthfulness, light, and clarity."[6] It is this degrading of the Reformation's intent to make the world into a site of God's agency and a place in which the believer is made holy that led to, among other things, a minimization of the role of the church in the daily lives of believers.[7]

In claiming the world beyond the church as the preferred arena for the believer's sanctification, the unintended consequence emerged that church and world were seen as polarities. In order to embrace the liberty of grace, of salvation by God independent of any church mediation, the life in the world was conceived of as necessarily *independent of the community of faith*. The now commonplace observation about a free-market world, that you can have as much freedom as you can buy, emerged in part from this understanding of the freedom of the believer in society as an individual characteristic, unrestrained by the dictates of the church. And so, following the Reformation, a

6. Dietrich Bonhoeffer, *Ethics*, trans. Reinhard Krauss, Charles C. West, and Douglass W. Stott, Dietrich Bonhoeffer Works 6 (Minneapolis: Fortress, 2005), 114–15.

7. Bonhoeffer, *Ethics*, 115. For a more contested version of this same argument, see Brad Gregory, *The Unintended Reformation: How a Religious Revolution Secularized Society* (Cambridge, MA: Belknap, 2015).

paradox emerged: it is the church-community's proclamation and practice that gives orientation to the self, but it is in the world that we embrace the vocations that God has for the believer. We cannot do without departing, but how do we do this without falling into the trap named above? How are we to live apart without once again turning the gift of freedom into isolation's iron mandate, dividing our gathered life from our days apart from the church-community? Can we draw together the "day apart" with the "day together"?

Silence and Restrained Speech: The Mark of the Day Apart

Knitting these "days" back together begins with how we conceive of speech. If the mark of the community is its speech—the hearing of Scripture, the singing of the common song, the words of confession, the prayers of the people—the mark of day apart is silence.[8] But by "silence," we do not mean the absence of sound but the refusal to overcome the words coming from the world rather than hearing them well. At work, for example, I engage new processes, new regimes of knowledge and patterns of behavior that press in on my mind and habits. To go into the world and *not* hear them would not only be imprudent for me as a worker but also would be to deny, as we have already seen, that the Christ of the church is the Lord of creation, calling all the world to its center. In work, in our days apart from the gathered church-community, I must pay attention not only because I am called to love the world that God has made but also because unless I listen during time in the world, I cannot hear what God might wish for the church to hear in these days, and will miss what God wishes to be drawn into the community to be healed. To begin with listening here is not to disavow the Word celebrated when we are gathered but to acknowledge that the same Word who calls the church to worship is the one who calls us into a world where the Word is not the dominant voice.

In the Epistle to Diognetus, an early Christian apology, the author spends time distinguishing between what Christians believe and what is held by Greeks and by Jews, carving out a new way of the Christian

8. Bonhoeffer, *Life Together*, 84.

in the world. But in distinguishing Christian practice from the other alternatives, the author introduces an important caveat—Christians are remarkably unspectacular in how they inhabit the world:

> For Christians are not distinguished from the rest of humanity by country, language, or custom. For nowhere do they live in cities of their own, nor do they speak some unusual dialect, nor do they practice an eccentric life-style. This teaching of theirs has not been discovered by the thought and reflection of ingenious men, nor do they promote any human doctrine, as some do. But while they live in both Greek and barbarian cities, as each one's lot was cast, and follow the local customs in dress and food and other aspects of life, at the same time they demonstrate the remarkable and admittedly unusual character of their own citizenship. They live in their own countries, but as aliens; they participate in everything as citizens, and endure everything as foreigners. Every foreign country is their fatherland, and every fatherland is foreign.[9]

This relationship is possible, he adds, because "what the soul is in the body, Christians are in the world. The soul is dispersed through all the members of the body, and Christians are scattered through all the cities of the world." Here, the epistle is not resorting to an invisible image of the church, submerged and silent in the world, but instead to a church that is present in creation, being altered by it, suffering it, as an imitation of Christ: "But perhaps [God] sent [Christ], as a man might suppose, to rule by tyranny, fear, and terror? Certainly not! On the contrary, he sent him in gentleness and meekness, as a king might send his son who is a king; he sent him as God; he sent him as a man to men. When he sent him, he did so as one who saves by persuasion, not compulsion, for compulsion is no attribute of God."[10]

In our day apart, our "silence" is one of unlearning the ways in which we defend ourselves against the "body" of the world that we share with creation. It is in this space that we take the disciplines and words, promises, Scriptures, and prayers of the gathered body into the folds of creation, to learn in new and intimate ways what they

9. The Epistle to Diognetus 5, in *The Apostolic Fathers: Greek Texts and English Translations*, ed. Michael W. Holmes (Grand Rapids: Baker, 1999), 541.
10. Epistle to Diognetus 7, pp. 543–45.

mean. Silence, likewise, does not mean the refusal to speak but rather the willingness to be present and listen for the words that need to be called forth from us that match the world's specific wounds: prophecy, consolation, lament, or praise. The presumption of listening begins here as we listen to what is being said, suffering it and offering our speech in the way that the wound of the world can hear, creating a multiplicity of true ways into the one gospel.

Relearning Speech

In the gathered community, so much speech is provided for us already—the Scriptures, prayers, the sermon—and so the day apart might be viewed as the day when I get my say, the day when I can distinguish myself from the community. What we are as creatures is inseparable from the communities that shape us, but it does not follow that what we need is to wrest ourselves away from the community and stake our claim: in Christ, we are *already* those who cannot be interchanged with someone else without loss, as if what was most important about you being you was your agency or your voice. To be a creature of God is not to be a collection of impersonal principles but rather to be a creature that God has intentionally created, a creature whose being and significance cannot be lost, even if we never added a single word to the common word except "Amen."[11] It is on this basis, then, that we are able to act in the world in a way as a gift of, and not as a defense against, the community.

In embracing silence—both in terms of listening to the world and in terms of reflecting on the words spoken in the day together—as our default way in this day, not only are we living in imitation of the Word who has called us into creation but we are learning that our day apart is not the counterpoint of being together, in two ways. First, in silence, I am resisting making my voice an equal to the community. While, at some level, the question of individual influence is

11. On this point, see Demetrios Harper's *The Analogy of Love: St. Maximus the Confessor and the Foundations of Ethics* (Yonkers, NY: St. Vladimir's Seminary Press, 2019), 162–63: as creations by the Word, we exist as what can be described as "nodes" of nature, those configurations of human nature that are intentional gifts by the Word.

unavoidable within any group, what is important here is that—when apart (because isolation is our default position)—I may be tempted to accord my own thoughts equal weight with those of the community. This is not to say that in the church there are not unrecognized gifts that go unreceived or that groups cannot fall into hegemony and tyranny: what is meant here is simply that what I am is a member of the body, a member whose life is tied into that of the community, and that the insights, gifts, strengths, and experiences I bear as a part of what I am are called by God into that body. If, in the day alone, my singular wisdom becomes equal to the weight of the community, I would be simply restating isolation's principle: the community may add counsel and comfort, but they are unnecessary, for I am ultimately on my own to hear the Word of the Lord.

But secondly, prioritizing silence allows the Word, rather than my own words, to have the first place within the shape of my day. As the Word comes to me both through the Scripture and through the words of others I encounter in those days apart from the church-community, my own words, insights, and plans find their place—not that I become the judge of the church-community who is not with me now but that my voice finds its standing alongside the voices of others: I begin to see how my ordinary life fits or has dissonance with the gathered community, how the words we share together flesh themselves out in the contours of work, family, and mission that are given to me in these days. When I start with silence, my sense of judgment can start anew, being reframed by what I have heard with others.

If one danger of the day apart is that we will think ourselves finally freed of the community, the equal and opposite danger is that in the day apart, we will long for the community so that we will not *have to* speak. The point of the day alone will be lost if we fall off the other edge and think of the gifts that are clarified and honed in these days alone as worthless.[12] For the prayers that you offer alongside the body of Christ are the prayers that *you* have been given to pray, and it is *this* voice and this voice alone that God has given you so that you may praise God. It is one thing to have our voice added to those of

12. Bonhoeffer, *Life Together*, 85: "Silence before the Word leads to proper hearing and thus also to proper speaking of God's Word at the right time."

others in unison and to have our voice shaped by the presence and challenge of others, but it is a different thing to simply adopt the voices of another as one's own.

In order to speak well as a member of the community—neither substituting one's witness for that of the community (in isolation from it) nor muting one's own voice entirely (isolating oneself from the community)—one must learn how to be alone well. This is not something to apologize for: being flung out into the world of work, family, and society apart from fellow Christians is not a lesser vocation. While it is in the day together that we encounter Christ in the bread and wine, in the preached Word, and in the presence of the body of Christ, the day alone compels us to follow Christ into the world in *mission*.

In Bonhoeffer's often-cited comments about how the world had "come of age,"[13] we find him noting that the world no longer responds to the Christian gospel, because it understands God to simply be that for which there is not yet an explanation.[14] The way forward for Christian witness, he writes, is not one of "conservative restoration," for there is no going back to the world before the Enlightenment; there is no going back to a world in which society takes its cues from the church.[15] As we go into the world, we go without abandoning the form of our community together, yet we do not go out in order to help the church survive, to weaponize the church against the world, but to reconcile all of creation to Christ, the Christ who is already present to us in the world.

The day apart is characterized by any number of opportunities for hearing the world and bringing the community's gospel into our places of work and of social obligation, and manifold words have been written on this. But we must attend to how the disciplines of our day together—in particular (1) our reading of Scripture, (2) prayer, (3) intercession for others, and (4) acts of mission and mercy—are exercised while we are apart in such a way that they do not divide us from the gathered body. It is these four points—a composite life of prayer and action—that help make the day apart a time of deepening

13. Bonhoeffer, *Letters and Papers*, 389.
14. Bonhoeffer, *Letters and Papers*, 426.
15. Bonhoeffer, *Letters and Papers*, 429.

our relation to the community of the church and not, on the one hand, a time spent in some sphere separate from the church or, on the other hand, a time of isolation that we endure until we can be rejoined to the church.

Meditation on Scripture: Finding the Self in Christ, toward the Body

It has become increasingly unfashionable to speak of "personal devotion" with respect to reading Scripture, but this is owing, I think, in no small part to the isolating and individualized tendencies associated with private Bible study.[16] In chapter 2, we described the trajectory that occurs here, with the Bible as that which is put into the hands of the individual for individual edification, a trajectory that ends in the dissolution of the church as in any way necessary for us to hear the voice of God. But if the reading of Scriptures together is one of the hallmarks of our gathered time, then the reading of Scripture alone belongs to the day apart as well. The intent here is the same: to be knit together into the body of Christ.

With all of the risks associated with the Scriptures in the hands of the private reader, it is not as if reading Scripture has never been subject to these kinds of fractures: even in the earliest centuries of the church, readings of Scripture were frequently contested by interpreters (independent of times the consensus readings were challenged by heretics!).[17] But in the interpretive decisions of an Origen, a Tertul-

16. Part of the question here, as we have been describing it, is the divorce of the reading of Scripture from the common life of the church, the roots of which are complex. For an account of this history, see Scott Hahn and Benjamin Wiker, *Politicizing the Bible: The Roots of Historical Criticism and the Secularization of Scripture* (New York: Herder & Herder, 2013), and, for the more modern inheritance of this legacy, Michael Legaspi, *The Death of Scripture and the Rise of Biblical Studies* (Oxford: Oxford University Press, 2011).

17. As Frances Young describes it in *God's Presence: A Contemporary Recapitulation of Early Christianity* (Cambridge: Cambridge University Press, 2013), 36: "Major Christian doctrines held in common across the denominations emerged through argument and deduction from scripture, communal decision having been made at key moments in history when scripture's ambiguities needed clarifying." The key example of this dynamic is the interpretive debates surrounding Scripture and the doctrine of the Trinity, as recounted by R. P. C. Hanson's *The Search for the Christian Doctrine*

lian, or an Augustine, concern about how their personal readings were contributing to a common, catholic reading was foregrounded: if the Scriptures were given to the gathered people of God first, our personal readings are governed by this concern and will ultimately return to this.

In a world in which that cat is out of the bag, however, with the Bible the single most produced book in the publishing industry worldwide, one possibility is to simply negate all personal Scripture reading and relocate Scripture to its public home.[18] But let us consider an alternative. The point in our personal reading of Scripture is not to deny the privatizing dangers that come with it but to begin in a different place: rather than mining the Scriptures for something for "personal application" (with the Scriptures as raw data to be assimilated), we begin in a posture of *listening* as we allow Scripture to interrogate us, a posture consistent with what we saw in the mode of Scripture reading when we were gathered. Put differently, if we are now gifted with so many Bibles, the possibility of fragmentation now becomes a chance to reclaim an important Reformation principle of Scripture reading: we do not ask what the Scriptures are speaking to others, or even ask questions of the Scriptures, but listen for the direct address of God, to have God confront and address us as the one who wills for all believers to be as one in their confessions, their prayers, and their witness.[19]

In listening for the voice of God—beginning in silence instead of speech—we are listening for the same God we hear when gathered. By sitting with the words of Scripture, expecting that they will speak

---

of God (Edinburgh: T&T Clark, 1998) and Lewis Ayres's revision of this history in *Nicaea and Its Legacy* (Oxford: Oxford University Press, 2004).

18. I am sympathetic to Stanley Hauerwas's proposal in *Unleashing the Scripture: Freeing the Bible from Captivity to America* (Nashville: Abingdon, 1993), 15–16, where he writes, "Most North American Christians assume that they have a right, if not an obligation, to read the Bible. I challenge that assumption. No task is more important than for the Church to take the Bible out of the hands of individual Christians in North America. . . . I am aware that this suggestion cannot help appearing authoritarian and elitist. I am not, however, particularly bothered by such characterizations, because I am challenging the very presumption that communities can exist without authority." As I will detail, however, there are potent reasons for retaining this practice of personal reading of Scripture.

19. Bonhoeffer, *Life Together*, 87.

directly to us, we are not expecting that what will be spoken to us will be words of *comfort or ease*. Rather, like the call to the disciples or to Zacchaeus, the call of Christ to us through the Scriptures will be that which pulls us out of hiding and calls us into the fellowship of Christ, to be changed.

In the early church, the Scriptures—by their very nature—opened themselves up in polyphonic fashion, revealing depths upon meditation rather than a singular point. For the ancient church, it was assumed that this happened because the Scriptures are the revelation of God and therefore speak comprehensively of the healing that Christ brings to the human condition: body, mind, soul, social environment, and more.[20] Indeed, the Scriptures, speaking to who God is and what we are before God, *welcome* this kind of polyphonic reading, for in this polyphony—the intimate address of the high and low of creation—the Word seeks out all corners of the deep. This polyphony of the Scriptures was knit together as a singular work for the earliest readers, reflecting the unity of the church as one body of Christ. This unity of reading was predicated on the unity of the body: God creates the harmony of Scripture, and thus of the church, even when the Scriptures are read in diverse places.[21]

And so, in our listening to the Scriptures, they address us as the multifaceted creatures that we are, calling for our transformation in mind, body, soul, and heart: If it is as bodily creatures that we are joined to one another in the church, why would we shy away from these dimensions in our personal reading? The particular fragilities that the Scriptures seek out and speak to are not to be apologized

20. On the ways in which the ancient church read the Scriptures as revealing multiple layers and thus having polyphonic meaning, see Hans Boersma, *Scripture as Real Presence: Sacramental Exegesis in the Early Church* (Grand Rapids: Baker Academic, 2020).

21. John J. O'Keefe and R. R. Reno, *Sanctified Vision: An Introduction to Early Christian Interpretation of the Bible* (Baltimore: Johns Hopkins University Press, 2005), 125–39, rightly questions whether the vaunted "rule of faith," binding diverse readings of Scripture together, was as solid as interpreters such as Irenaeus thought, and instead points to the common sanctifying bodily practices of the church as the golden thread that created commonality over divergences in reading. On the ways in which this scriptural polyphony found resonance with the polyphony of Christian witness, see Barry Harvey, *Taking Hold of the Real: Dietrich Bonhoeffer and the Profound Worldliness of Christianity* (Eugene, OR: Cascade Books, 2015), 234–68.

for, but acknowledged and welcomed. But the ways in which the Scriptures speak to the various elements of our lives are not the end toward which God's speech is ordered: The telos here is not that I would come to be actualized by myself (and thus, always have to find ways to be knit back together to the community). The telos is that Christ would seek out that which is damaged in the world, that all of what I am and what my world consists of would be knit back together. God's address to me qua me is to draw me out of myself and rejoin me into the good work of God.

And so, as much as possible, our habits of reading the Scriptures apart from one another should reflect this reality, focusing on longer passages, narratively pointing us to the reality that today's readers are part of a larger story: we are joined to the work of God in Christ that preceded us and that joins our little community of readers to the larger and older work of God in Christ, a work that will go on into eternity. In listening to the Scriptures, we pray to be opened up by the Spirit, so that our evasion of God might be undone.[22]

There are, of course, many ways to avoid this wildness of God's address, by appealing to the singularity of Scripture over against this more polyphonic approach. One way is to retreat into an "objective" reading of Scripture, avoiding the Word's direct address; in this approach, the Scripture possesses only one meaning, and after discovering that, the work of reading and hearing has been done and all that remains is to hide behind that singular reading. Another way of avoiding this polyphony is to move directly into action instead of remaining with the Scripture for what God might speak through it, which might be contrary to my first instincts. In moving immediately to action, we short-circuit the very process by which we become wise and prudential people: courses of action emerge as the consequence of deliberation, and in the day apart from one another, deliberation over what to do occurs as I give deliberation the time due it.[23] The

22. Bonhoeffer, *Life Together*, 88: "As Mary 'pondered in her heart,' . . . so as we meditate, God's Word desires to enter in and stay with us. . . . Then it will do its work in us, *often without our being aware of it*" (emphasis mine).

23. For an excellent discussion of deliberation, the moral agent, and the conditions of deliberation, see Oliver O'Donovan, *Finding and Seeking*, vol. 2 of *Ethics as Theology* (Grand Rapids: Eerdmans, 2014).

movement to immediate action, however, conceived of as "my task before God," can frequently be a species of the isolated individual making the best of their situation, operating only from within their intuitions as they seek a way forward in response to God's call.

The practical action in response to God's call through Scripture will come, but to act, we must first hear—be addressed by the same Word that the church scattered throughout the world is being addressed by. In listening to the address of Christ, we are listening first for God, in a way that first does not elicit our action but instead puts our offers of actions *at risk*. For in our offers of action, we are frequently evading the simple and clear word of God that seeks us out: instead of following directly, we offer to take care of our obligations, to plow our fields, to bury our dead—and in making these offers, we refuse to be called out of our self-imposed obligations and all the safety that comes with them.

In meditating on Scripture, even alone, we join our listening to the listening that the people of God have done across time, joining with Israel, the church past, and the church present.[24] It is humbling to know that, when it is time to do something in light of Scripture, I do what I do as part of a great body of hearers, spread out across time and space, not as the bearer of a private message that has no greater context than myself. What I hear from God in the day apart I am invited to bring back into the body, for the sake of the formative work that happens when we are together, for Christ is both present in and through the Word meditated and the Word preached. Like all living bodies, the church-community is made alive by that which comes to it through its openings and pores.[25] For the church to be denied these

24. Consider Dietrich Bonhoeffer, *Prayerbook of the Bible: An Introduction to the Psalms*, trans. James H. Burtness, in *Life Together; Prayerbook of the Bible*, Dietrich Bonhoeffer Works 5 (Minneapolis: Fortress, 1996), 165: "We pray these psalms when we look upon everything that God once did for God's people as having been done for us, when we confess our guilt and the divine grace, when on the basis of God's former wonderful works we hold God to promises made and pray for fulfillment, and when we finally see the entire history of God's people with their God fulfilled in Jesus Christ, through whom we have been helped and will be helped."

25. The body of Christ/human body analogy is instructive for the church-community's operations, not only for Paul (1 Cor. 6:18–20) but from an ecological perspective: the church's health (physically and spiritually) is integrally related to the

external words is for us to seal the body off from nourishment; it also, to follow the analogy, forecloses the possibility that the church could remove from itself toxins and illness because of the gifts that come from outside of it. Inevitably, what I see in the Scriptures will be something that speaks to the conditions of my own life, but the point is not to find in Scripture something that can be irreducibly *my* gift; the point is, through that, to become a gift to the community.

Prayer: Finding the Self in Scripture's Vision

Scripture, which helps us to name the world and calls out of us that which we would prefer to hide, leads us as we turn to prayer. As we read it, it becomes the basis of our prayers, guiding both their content and their direction. In meditating on Scripture, we turn to prayer, but prayer here is not a return to the self—once again, isolation stands ready to enter in by letting us focus on our own condition, our needs, what is ours as opposed to others: to do so would be to "become the victims of our own emptiness."[26] If we assume that Scripture is that which we *receive*, but that in prayer we add our own resources to Scripture, we forget that it is through the Spirit (by whom we receive the Word) that we are being reformed and retrained to add our voices to Scripture.

Not all of the things that we intuitively reach for in prayer are those that should be at the center of our prayers, but surprisingly, the concerns that the Scriptures embrace range from the celestial to the mundane, from the deeply passionate to the coolly rational. In prayer, we do not set aside some elements of what it means to be God's creatures; rather, by praying with Scripture's leading, we find out *how* these elements are taken up by God. In prayer we lay out all that we are, with Scripture as our lead, looking not for some aspect of our bodily life to be left out but for all of it to find its place in the prayers we offer. Accordingly, it is with good reason that when liturgical prayers offer time for the prayers of the individual, and *I*

---

world's social and moral ecology. On this, see Pope Francis, *Laudato Si': On Care for Our Common Home* (Huntington, IN: Our Sunday Visitor, 2015), paragraphs 79–100.

26. Bonhoeffer, *Life Together*, 84.

have opportunity to offer prayer for myself and my concerns, that time comes after prayers of penitence and pardon: what I most need is to be reintegrated into the body, to come home. Only then can I find my way to praying well for myself.

Through prayer, guided by the concerns of Scripture, we are being led ultimately beyond our own concerns and beyond the world as we wish it to be, and back toward the body of Christ, scattered now but waiting to be gathered. In her essay on prayer, the mystic Simone Weil puts it this way: prayer is more like schoolwork than like a conversation, in that in schoolwork, we are learning to pay loving attention to an object. As we give ourselves to the dynamics of handwriting, or math, or science, we are learning to appreciate it as we pay attention to it; prayer, likewise, is a learning to pay attention to God and not ourselves.[27] When (and not *if*) our prayers drift back toward a contemplation of ourselves, it is not a sign of our failure in prayer but an opportunity for reincorporation, for the self is part of what is rightly to be prayed for. Prayer, when led by Scripture, links together the intimacies of our lives with the corporate work of God in the church. For when a person prays, they are not so much asking to be extinguished as they are asking to be brought fully to life, so that they might find their communion with the work of God beyond themselves.

To return to Paul Griffiths's insights on the nature of being a bodily person, we are creatures of flesh, which is to say that we are creatures who are torn apart only at the risk of destroying what we are: that which is severed from the living ceases to be flesh and becomes instead inanimate matter, unless they are reincorporated into the living body.[28] The human in prayer is not meant to be a divided human, with those parts lopped off that are somehow unworthy to be redeemed: those aspects of our own bodily life—discarded dreams, halfway-conscious desires, aberrant thoughts—are all things that God wishes to redeem. If it is in prayer that we are joined to the community of Christ, then we leave elements of ourselves out of our prayer to the degree that

27. Simone Weil, "Attention and Will," in *Gravity and Grace* (London: Routledge, Taylor and Francis, 2002), 116–22.

28. Paul J. Griffiths, *Christian Flesh* (Stanford, CA: Stanford University Press, 2018), 13.

we think that somehow those things are not within God's purview to make whole, a gift for others.

Intercession: Finding the Self with Others in Prayer

When we turn in prayer from contemplating our own lives to offering up the lives of others, the act of prayer joins us to others and to God. Apart from this dimension of prayer, our prayers remain orbiting our own thoughts and concerns. To be sure, Scripture, providing the frame of not only how we pray but also what we pray for, begins with what we are and with whom we love, but it will not leave us there.

In praying for others, most naturally, we begin with the ones who are closest and most familiar to us. The ones we know the best are the ones who first come to mind and are the ones that we frequently owe the most to.[29] But in keeping with the aim of our prayer—that we are joined to the community of Christ—here, we must ask whether beginning prayer for those who are naturally closest to us does not repeat a key problem of community: the desire to create a community in my own image. For if my prayer—and thus my active joining to the community who is apart from me—occurs under the sign of those things that are closest to my mind and heart, the community that appears to me in prayer is one of my own making, one ordered in my own image of loves and affections.

This temptation, however, reveals a very real and valuable dimension of creaturely life: there is no place to begin prayer except through the place where one's own body is. We can pray only as the embodied, storied creatures that we are, not as some idealized version of a human. To demand some kind of transcendent position for our prayers is to demand that somehow we pray as other than grounded

---

29. The question of proximity in ethics is a perennially difficult one, emphasizing what we owe and to whom in a world of finite resources. Traditionally, the question has turned on not simply geographic but relational entanglements: we owe more to our proximate neighbors not simply because of geographic but because of interpersonal obligations, histories, forms of exchange, and social bonds. In a globalized world, however, demarking what counts as local and proximate becomes decidedly more difficult. For an overview and introduction to the issues here, see David Hollenbach, *The Common Good and Christian Ethics* (Cambridge: Cambridge University Press, 2002).

human beings who have real commitments and concerns.[30] And so, I begin praying for others where I am.

When we begin in this way, praying for others, spurred on by our affections for them, we must recall that, in Christ, they do not exist for my love or because of their virtue toward me but because they are those who are loved by Christ.[31] This is radical in two ways. First, those whom we would most naturally pray for, those who are most naturally valuable to us, are those whom we see now first as *forgiven sinners*. Set aside are those evaluations of my children that are built on my love for them, transfigured by seeing them as those whom God loves. I set aside praying for my friends solely because they are my friends, those whose faces I look forward to seeing or whose words bring me joy; I pray for them because they are redeemed creatures of Christ whom I am joined with eternally only because of God. The hallowing of the world in prayer begins with the hallowing of those nearest to me.

But second, those we naturally pray for, because of their intimacy to us, become those whom we can likewise forgive, not allowing friendship and affection to obscure the need for forgiveness to mediate the best of bonds. It is not the slights of a stranger that cut us the deepest, but those of a friend. In setting aside a person's goodness and praying for them as one for whom Christ has died, not only are the best parts of them transfigured but the wounds that they bring are also reframed. Intercession, beginning in the intimate and valuable folds of our lives, expands outward into those intimate but harmful folds and finally to those folds of our life that we might be less inclined to include in our prayers. For when we intercede, beginning with what is closest to us, we find ourselves confronted not only with those we love the most but also with those who have concretely hurt us the most: the one whom we worship with but who has something against us, the coworker in the world of work with whom we share meals, the supervisor who has belittled us.

In praying through the vision of Scripture, then, I am not meant to negate these natural loves but to expand this circle, from familiar

30. Griffiths, *Christian Flesh*, 6.
31. Bonhoeffer, *Life Together*, 90: "In intercessory prayer the face that may have been strange and intolerable to me is transformed into the face of one for whom Christ died, the face of a pardoned sinner."

to stranger, and from stranger to enemy. When I join with the Psalms, for example, I can pray categorically that "the hope of the poor" not be taken away,[32] but the intent is that when I pray, that category is filtered through the poor I actually am touched by. In beginning with the actual poor, for example, I am invited to pray, through the concrete, for all of the concreteness I do not know.[33]

Some of these who it is strange for me to pray for are those who are estranged from me—those whose lives are alien to me or opposed to me. Intercession takes us here as well. For the community of Christ, as we have seen, is composed not on the basis of those I have affection for but of those for whom Christ has died. Such prayer—for both those we love and those we do not yet—is something we "train ourselves to set a regular time during the day for," for learning to see people in this way runs against some of our dispositions.[34] It is in learning to pray alone for the ones of the body that I hate that I am brought home from the far country, not by praying for the ones that I already love. Learning to pray is a matter of habit, for we must learn *how* to pay attention in our prayer and to let God do the work in us that only God can do.

Work and Mercy: The Day Apart Tested and Expanded

The "day apart" is not only prayer, meditation, and Scripture but also labor. The "day apart" and the disciplines of that day are not only about extending the prayers of the community into the intimate folds of our daily life but also about expanding the work of our gathered worship into the endless spaces of the world. In an earlier discussion, we named the role of mission within the day together, but it is important that we do not make a hard distinction between this and

32. Psalm 9:18: "For the needy shall not always be forgotten, nor the hope of the poor perish forever."

33. For this, see Michelle Ferrigno Warren, *The Power of Proximity: Moving beyond Awareness to Action* (Downers Grove, IL: InterVarsity, 2017). I have written on this particular dynamic in Bonhoeffer with application to immigration in "Bearing the Impossible Present: Bonhoeffer, Illegality, and the Witness for Migrants," *Bonhoeffer Legacy: An International Journal* (forthcoming).

34. Bonhoeffer, *Life Together*, 91.

labor: the divide that we posit between church and world and the one we posit between "mission" and "work" are related.

The work, the laboring that we do apart from the church-community, is related to the day together in that what is done apart is an extension of the corporate work that Christ is working out, both positively and negatively. The work of the day alone is not only for testing and proving what has been done in the day together: the work we do alone is (like the labor of the day together) the work of *mission*. By mission, I do not mean solely evangelism, that what we do apart from the church is to persuade people to come to church. Rather, what we do in extending the work of prayer to the day apart is to extend the kingdom of God through *being the image of Christ's body in the world*.

Because isolation and separation are central to what sin does to creation, we cannot thus conceive of the work of mission as that which conveys the work of God in a way that is calibrated toward the autonomous individual, accommodating the reconciling work of God to the conditions of isolation. As we saw with prayer, we pray not to become more of ourselves *apart* from the work of God in the church but so that we may be drawn into what God is doing with us all together. Likewise, what we image in the world through our work, through our conversation, through our acts of mercy is *not* my individual gifts or testimony but how God in Christ is bringing reconciliation and wholeness to a world that can only think of wholeness as making me authentically *me* over against *you*.

One immediate difficulty here is that the context of work and ordinary life is freighted by a condition of fragmentation that alters all things within it: our modes of economic exchange.[35] The ways in which we work, relate to our neighbors, gather associationally, or send our children to school—these all fall under the specter of the governing limits of economic relations. Whether our children play

35. Bruce Rogers-Vaughn's *Caring for Souls in a Neoliberal Age* (New York: Palgrave Macmillan, 2016) emphasizes the manner in which economic stresses not only fray social bonds but create forms of intangible suffering, such that one is afflicted but unable to identify particular agents causing that suffering. For a practical guide for congregations on these questions, see Tim Conder and Dan Rhodes, *Organizing Church: Grassroots Practices for Embodying Change in Your Congregation, Your Community, and Your World* (Danvers, MA: Chalice, 2017).

in a private soccer league, or we have the ability to take off work on the weekends to eat with our neighbors, or we can be involved with the local parent-teacher association—all of these opportunities are at some level economically driven in ways that form associations with some persons and not others, sorting society in ways which are calibrated more and more frequently according to class. And so, expanding the mission of our gathered life into our work in the world requires attending to the ways in which economic exchange, presumptions, and limits shape these encounters and learning how these presumptions shape our exchanges with one another to be transactional in nature.[36]

If the church-community exists as a body whose members operate together, materially consisting of weak and strong bound together in Christ, then the Christian in the world operates against these limits in both acknowledgment of the ways we are shaped by them and in challenge of them. In gathering with our neighbors, we must become accustomed to asking not just, What shall we do? but, Why is it that our neighbors are unable to get together? If, like myself, your work day runs from morning to afternoon during the week, your imagination might immediately run to a dinner after the workday has ended, forgetting that your neighbors are frequently working swing shifts, gig labor, and long weekend nights. Joining with my neighbors thus takes the form not only of accommodating to the schedules that their work demands but also of advocating for more just work practices that allow my neighbors to have the Sabbath rest they need. If loving our neighbors involves caring for the local schools, it means both helping to fulfill classroom needs and working for avenues for participation of parents without the luxury to take off during the work week, ensuring that participation in the good of children is not limited to those who benefit from often invisible economic arrangements. The union of the weak and strong—intrinsic to the church-community—bears itself out,

36. Much has been written on the question of impingements of economics on social life, particularly on the way in which religion uncritically contributes to these arrangements. Kathryn Tanner's *Christianity and the New Spirit of Capitalism* (New Haven: Yale University Press, 2019) updates the literature, which was largely indebted to the work of Max Weber, by emphasizing the way in which short-term investment and financialization encourage relational behaviors that are tactical, short term, and transactional.

then, in what Karl Barth referred to as "parables of the kingdom," living metaphors that serve to remind the hearer of that which animates them.[37] If the risk that missions perpetually runs is that it will replicate corrupted and isolating internal assumptions out into the world—whether of the false divisions of race, economics, or gender—then it is all the more important that our approach to the world attend not simply to drawing a person into the faith but also to drawing them into the *communion of Christ*, enacting parables of life together.

The day apart conceives of mission as that which occurs within the folds of the ordinary, not as that which is extraordinary: mission is what happens as the Christian extends and expands the reach of their life together into the cracks of the world, not what happens when the ordinary world is put on pause. For isolation and division are everywhere, and the mission of God expands outward from where the body of Christ is, drawing all things into the orbit of Christ's body. Because the church is not built on one sector of society or one class, the redemptive outward work of Christ will proceed in a way that encompasses all of the world as the church scatters during the week.

The attention given to the "day apart" is missional attention in the end. For the formation of the church's members continues beyond the time of gathering, drawing new corners into the gathered life of the church. The body of Christ changes and expands as the day apart happens, and the world is enlivened, hallowed, and renewed as it is drawn into the day together. In the end, the corporate work of God in Christ is of one piece with the separate works that are done: the isolation of sin wants to cordon off some sector of creation that is autonomously "the world," but the day together creates myriad missionaries who proceed into the world in the day apart to refuse this separation.

Turning Back to Gathering

The Word that we hear in the day apart and in the day together is of one piece: there is not a competition between the words that Christ in

37. Karl Barth, "The Christian Community and the Civil Community," §27, in *Karl Barth: Theologian of Freedom*, ed. Clifford C. Green (Minneapolis: Fortress, 1991), 289.

the Scriptures speaks to us in solitude and those that are heard when we are together. The Word made flesh, who proceeds into the world and who created all that is, does reveal the God who has made all things and who desires that all things return to God. In this whole-sale redemption of creation, we have seen that the regnant isolation that characterizes sin must not be uprooted by dividing church from creation or dividing the believers from their neighbors, for it is for the sake of creation that Christ has come.

But it is not enough to address the liturgical practices by which we undergo a theological therapy for the sin that must be drawn out of us like a poison. We must also turn our attention to the ordinary practices and habits that, if left unexamined, will likewise foster in us isolation—practices and habits that we develop through our careful attention to reading Scripture, praying, and singing. To these ordinary practices of the Christian life we now turn.

Six

Renewing the Shape
of Ministry

Thus far, much of our exploration has been about the way our practices as church are not for the sake of escaping isolation but for the cultivation of an ethos—a journey into salvation—in which isolation is replaced by community, a community that attends to the complex relationship between its inner life, its mission, and its scattering. The objection can be raised to this vision, though, that it is too heroic, one fit for the extraordinary and not for the ordinary.[1] In one sense, there is no need to apologize for being aspirational, to set

1. There has been a great deal of recent literature emphasizing the need for a retrieval of ordinary virtue as opposed to "heroic virtue," the latter of which tends to assume perfect conditions for moral growth. For two such accounts, see in particular Todd May, *A Decent Life: Morality for the Rest of Us* (Chicago: University of Chicago Press, 2019); and Rebecca Stangl, *Neither Heroes nor Saints: Ordinary Virtue, Extraordinary Virtue, and Self-Cultivation* (Oxford: Oxford University Press, 2020). Within recent Bonhoeffer scholarship, Jennifer Moberly's *The Virtue of Bonhoeffer's Ethics: A Study of Dietrich Bonhoeffer's Ethics in Relation to Virtue Ethics* (Eugene, OR: Pickwick, 2013) is exemplary for its attention to this neglected theme. Bonhoeffer is, as we have seen, largely skeptical of Promethean projects of human perfection, attentive to the ways in which the pursuit of virtue and community was rooted in God's gifting.

into motion a trajectory of the church's common life that is beyond our present abilities and that we cannot presently see the complete form of. But these critiques raise an important point for Christians: our life together, morally speaking, is not a technique we employ in ideal situations but a common work that—if it accomplishes great things—is largely not our doing.[2]

And so, to speak of our life together, we must turn to the shape of ministry that the people have toward one another in ordinary life, the frame of our lives that sets the stage for whatever other "heroic" moments might approach us. The shape of ministry must be guided toward participating in Christ's renewal of the world, both inside the church and as the church expands this mission into the folds of the world. For the things that we do will shape our community; the virtues that we cultivate in our actions, Scripture knows, will be the shape of the community.[3]

To return to the distinction that we have made many times, the difference between a ministry that is framed by *isolation* and one that shapes a *church-community* is of great importance. And thus, in this chapter, we will explore two kinds of elements to the life of ordinary virtue: the negative and the positive, the habits that must be refrained from and those that must be enacted. For, to paraphrase the parable of Jesus, it is not enough to simply clean out the house of demons if nothing is put in its place (Luke 11:21–26). To simply clean out a house of vice without filling it once again with virtue—or in this case, to attend to practices of gathering and ministry apart from the ordinary practices of life together—is to simply defer the collapse of the house one more day. To rout out the spirit of isolation without

2. In framing the limits of individual agency in this way, I am not meaning to diminish the "costliness" of discipleship; rather, I am affirming the limits of our agency as having results that outstrip our ability to determine the results. If the results of our discipleship are "heroic," it is largely, I think, an accident of history that makes it so: the right actor and action at the right moment, in which the results produce a result beyond that which could be reasonably predicted.

3. It is here that Philip Turner, *Christian Ethics and the Church: Ecclesial Foundations for Moral Thought and Practice* (Grand Rapids: Baker Academic, 2015), 191–93, rightly emphasizes that this is not a heroic vision but one that must "make room for mediocrity," for virtue is not simply a matter of will but of moral luck, and of sometimes incompatible demands. On this last point, see Lisa Tessman, *Moral Failure: The Impossible Demands of Morality* (Oxford: Oxford University Press, 2015).

building up a community in Christ is only to keep the temptations of isolation at bay.

Practices amid Weak and Strong

Returning to a theme from chapter 4, let us begin these discussions of ordinary ministries of the community by recalling that the community is made of "the weak" and "the strong," by which we mean the manifold differences that exist within any congregation, some by nature and some by the invisible movement of sin-as-injustice. In the discussions of church practice, the distinctions of a church-community affected our understanding of how giftedness and ability operated, but here, these distinctions take a different cast and must be turned to again.

We are after forming a community in Christ, a work that is inefficient on its best days, and frequently, we align "effectiveness" and "gifting" in our thinking. As we saw in chapter 2, the temptations toward holding a community together on strength of personality and vision and the temptations of the demagogue are real. Likewise, here, eliding "strength of ability" with "gifting" is a temptation for the community to get to where it wants to go as fast as possible: the strong simply put isolation to the side for a moment rather than eradicating it.

The dangers of sublating the weak to the giftings of the strong are well documented, including making the weak into the image of the strong and imposing bourgeois standards of giftedness. But here we must also mine the dangers unique to those lacking influence within the community. Within the community of the church, the spirit of "who should be the greatest" is rarely absent, and in deceptive forms. The ones whose voices are the strongest or whose gifts are the greatest are the most obvious targets here, for they are the ones who can most easily shape the community to their own vision and wishes and, in doing so, kill the community.

But the *weak* also find a temptation arising here: they cannot overpower the strong, but they have available the possibility of leverage. This is not to say that in conflicts and in communities there are not actual victims: those who have been wronged have wounds that must be attended to. But let us attend to Bonhoeffer's comments here: "There are strong people and weak ones. If people are not strong, they immediately claim the right of the weak as their own and use it against the strong. People are talented and untalented, simple and difficult, devout and less devout, sociable and loners."[4] In each of these binaries, Bonhoeffer is driving at this point: whether one has influence or no influence, we all seek a different point of leverage, under the guise of "giftedness." *I am not gifted in leadership*, one might think, *but I am pious.* Or perhaps it appears in this form: *I am not the best singer, but I am doing the humble work of cleaning up that no one sees or appreciates.*

Real power dynamics that create real abuse in church communities are to be guarded against and attended to, whether perennial forms of bias codified into law and *regula* or unspoken forms of prejudice carried on as habits. But in the ongoing life of the church, those weaker in one area (and weakness has more forms than influence, power, and money) should be wary of reasoning who is greatest in the kingdom of God in a way that leverages themselves into power in a different way.[5]

This requires not just seeing the abuses of power that occur in church against the vulnerable but also reframing the notion of congregational power entirely: recognizing that both the weak and strong have agency, giftings, and power. Therefore, the "weapons of the weak," tactically leveraged, are to be cautioned against alongside the more obvious dangers: the strategic and broad-scale weapons of the strong.[6]

Throughout the Scriptures, the priority of the poor and weak is undeniable and pervasive.[7] The language of God leveling mountains and

---

4. Dietrich Bonhoeffer, *Life Together*, trans. Daniel W. Bloesch, in *Life Together; Prayerbook of the Bible*, Dietrich Bonhoeffer Works 5 (Minneapolis: Fortress, 1996), 93.

5. Bonhoeffer, *Life Together*, 96–97.

6. On this distinction between tactics and strategy and on the agency present in multiple parties of power struggles, see James C. Scott, *Domination and the Arts of Resistance* (New Haven: Yale University Press, 1990); and Scott, *Weapons of the Weak: Everyday Forms of Peasant Resistance* (New Haven: Yale University Press, 1985).

7. Though Christianity has always maintained great attention to the poor in terms of mercy, the rise of liberation theology in the twentieth century made this theme of

sending the powerful and the wealthy away empty-handed reminds us that within God's economy, inequity and injustice are incompatible with the kingdom of God. To say that God will give justice to the oppressed is good news. But the justice of God must not be mobilized for the establishment of a reversed form of isolation, in which the eye of the needle is closed off to the wealthy, with the gift of community offering them only judgment absent an opportunity for repentance.[8]

None of this eliminates the need for power analysis in church; too frequently, power operates invisibly, forming us to its demands and hidden privileges. What I am suggesting, however, is that power must be reframed as the will toward one another, rather than viewing power in its agonistic form. In the habits, both positive and negative, that follow, the struggle for self-justification persists: some by crafting an overarching strategy that will upend others, some by thinking tactically, finding their place of leverage. But in Christ's community, all are joined together ever and solely because of the work of Christ—they can offer their gifts without fear that their two mites are not enough and without hope that their large offerings make them superior.[9] To engage in the community is to recognize the common body that all have been called to and the common temptation that will approach all under different forms. And so, the discussion of ministry begins on level ground: the weak and the strong are both called to put off the temptation to leverage their place in the community. For this reason, then, we will begin with the negative—that which is to be avoided, allowing that to frame what must be done.

---

the poor's centrality to our theological reflection prominent as a centralizing hermeneutic. For this history and for a contemporary restatement, see Gustavo Gutiérrez and Cardinal Gerhard Ludwig Müller, *On the Side of the Poor: The Theology of Liberation* (Maryknoll, NY: Orbis Books, 2015).

8. Friedrich Nietzsche makes this accusation most clearly toward Christians, arguing that their historically low position was turned into a virtue to be able to weaponize against their culture. *On the Genealogy of Morals*, trans. Walter Kaufmann and R. J. Hollingdale, in *On the Genealogy of Morals; Ecce Homo* (New York: Vintage, 1989), 33–38.

9. The disparity of wealth within early church communities was the subject of much discussion and frequently of acute criticism that tied eternal states to how members dispossessed themselves of economic and social power. See Peter Brown, *Through the Eye of a Needle: Wealth, the Fall of Rome, and the Making of Christianity in the West, 350–550 AD* (Princeton: Princeton University Press, 2012).

Putting Off the Habits of Isolation

Holding One's Tongue

The first habit of the community emerges from the entry point that one person has to another: language. Actions are not self-interpreting, but require us to give accounts for why we have done this action or how that action is to be understood: the words of initiation with Communion are not simply to have something to say but to help the congregation know what is being done and why. Likewise, our words are the entry to our relationships to one another: a word spoken or withheld can be the way in which our life together becomes shaped. It is through our words that we have access to one another, most frequently in ways that perpetuate the boundaries between one person and another (through distinguishing the ways I am not you), and it is through our words that we then perpetuate the competition between persons (the ways in which I am gifted and you are not).

It is not always possible to know *positively* what to say: when someone is walking through tragedy, knowing what words of wisdom or grace are needed is an act of skill, and being able to positively offer these words begins by knowing what words are *not* to be shared. Therefore, we begin by refusing to let that which is evil—that which begins as an act of self-justification over against others—be expressed in words.[10] The other person is created as God's own creature, so any subtle steering through self-serving scrutiny, any desire to conform others into our own image, is to be guarded against.[11]

Recall again the first temptation in Genesis: in the words of the serpent, we see the temptation of *suspicion* toward the language we use in addressing one another, and we see the subsequent temptation to position ourselves through this suspicion over against God and all of God's creatures. By asking, "Did God really say that?" the serpent is not so much interested in getting humans to break God's law as it is interested in seducing them into placing God under judgment, injecting doubt about intention into the relationship between God and humanity.

10. Bonhoeffer, *Life Together*, 96.
11. Bonhoeffer, *Life Together*, 95.

In placing God's promise under judgment, the humans of Genesis 3 likewise place God's ordering and gifting of creation under judgment; with God displaced, my own vision of not only God but of all creation is elevated to the heart of reality. I become like God in the subtle temptation to engage in criticism, to position another person with my words, to put into language a new frame of reality that displaces and disposes of the one who is not yet at my disposal. We were made as creatures of language so that through our language we might have access to one another.[12] It is through language that we understand the world and through language that the church-community frequently comes undone.[13]

We are, by God's design, always mediated to one another—this is true even in paradise, Bonhoeffer writes, for if there were ever an occasion when we had unmediated access to one another, there would be an occasion when Christ was not at the center of who we are as creatures.[14] And so our access to one another in language was not for our criticism: I can never know beforehand how God's image should

12. See Rowan Williams, *The Edge of Words: God and the Habits of Language* (London: Bloomsbury Continuum, 2014), on the relation between God's relation to us through language and the implications of our own use of language. For an anthropological account of language and social relations, see Charles Taylor, *The Language Animal: The Full Shape of the Human Linguistic Capacity* (Cambridge, MA: Belknap, 2016). The difficulty with this emphasis that I am making on language is that it assumes that agency—and thus, recognition and personhood—is tied to language in ways that assume communicability, opening the possibility that those who exercise language differently, either through the inability to vocalize or those who speak in a different language, might remain alien to me. I take this not as a defeat of what I am describing here but rather as an opportunity for patience, to learn new communication, and possibly to hear a criticism of what I take to be the necessary and ordinary uses of language.

13. Dietrich Bonhoeffer, *Creation and Fall: A Theological Exposition of Genesis 1–3*, trans. Douglas Stephen Bax, Dietrich Bonhoeffer Works 3 (Minneapolis: Fortress, 1997), 113: "Truth against truth—God's truth against the serpent's truth. God's truth tied to the prohibition, the serpent's truth tied to the promise, God's truth pointing to my limit, the serpent's truth pointing to my unlimitedness—both of them truth, that is, both originating with God, God against God."

14. Recall Bonhoeffer's comments about the mediation that Christ has between even the partners in the most intimate of relationships. But also see his comments about the relation between the first people, in *Creation and Fall*, 98–99: "Knowing the other person as God's creature, simply as the other, as the other who stands beside me and constitutes a limit for me, and at the same time knowing that the other person is derived from me, from my life, and so loving the other and being loved by the other

appear in others but must operate first as the speaker of the Word, through whom I and another are bound together, and offer words in ways that offer promise, begin an inquiry, or evoke concern.[15] If behind the virtue of the weak is the same struggle for self-justification that the strong engage in more brazenly and openly, then the ultimate irony is that the weak ones in the community find themselves—by engaging in criticism of the strong—at risk in their pursuit of being shaped into the image of the crucified Son who is the center of the community. Our forms of language—our access to one another— are doorways of celebration and rejoicing, for in our speech, we find our first opportunity for communion with one another: in questions rather than accusations, inquiry instead of attack.

Our words, then, are meant to become acts of service, for we are judged by the same words that we speak to others. Evaluations of others originate from within my sense of self: I make statements and judgments before asking questions, seeking not to understand but to be understood, knowing that I already live up to the standard I am using. In using this measure, I already know how best to implement this judgment in my own life and thus am a step ahead of my fellow Christian. But if my words are *inquiries*, seeking out another whom I am not united to instead of leading with accusation, I let the words I speak be invitations in a commonly sought frame of our life together in Christ. If the weak and the strong do in fact exist in the same community, then our access to one another is obtained in a way that will not eradicate either the "weak" persons or the "strong," even if the absoluteness of these categories of weakness and strength comes under scrutiny.

Living in Meekness

To learn in our actions what characterizes our speech, we enter into a life of service to one another. Our actions—also refusing the power games of positioning our own reputation and gifts over against those of another—begin from the presumption that the other person is to be thought of first, even to the degree that one would negate

---

because the other is a piece of me—all that is for Adam the bodily representation of the limit that should make Adam's limit easier for Adam to bear."

15. Bonhoeffer, *Life Together*, 95.

thinking of oneself as wise. This is not the same as naming oneself objectively a fool: it is false humility to deny that one is gifted or experienced or wise when one *is* gifted or experienced or wise.[16] But by beginning our actions toward others in meekness—the knowledge of being forgiven by God—we are provided the proper moorings for offering our gifts and ourselves.

Our self-evaluation, for good or for ill, frequently turns on a criterion of judgment that assumes the validity of my self-knowledge: I know best what I am, what I have experienced, and what I have to offer. But in this mode, God is put into judgment, with our isolated conscience the arbiter, our judgments the mediator of right access to God, our self-knowledge the measure of how our gifts are to be received. But when we begin with our communion, our access to one another only by Christ, we have a new starting point for seeing the abilities of ourselves and of others: that what one is and what one has are to be given as a gift to others, and as such, the value of my gifts (and of my self) is *risked*: they are given but their reception is out of my hands. Meekness, in other words, is a way of acknowledging that what I am is interwoven with the good of others in Christ, from a common place of union in Christ. Humility follows here: who I am is not a titan of giftedness but a vehicle of blessing. Our gifts, abilities, and indeed experience are not meant for propping up our sense of self or gaining God's favor: they are for the neighbor's *needs*. In the same way that our words are for the benefit of our neighbors solely, so we measure what good we give by what our neighbors need and not solely by the depths that we might have to offer.[17]

The difficulty here is that when I begin from the presumption that what I have and the experience I have is for the good of others, the possibility opens up that my gifts and offerings will be unreceived and that my lifetime of experience and gifts will be left in shadows and unused. So here I must emphasize that to begin in meekness is not to invite others to abuse us or to go looking for opportunities to be abused but to expect that *when* we are overlooked or when our gifts go unused within a community, we consider again what sustains a

16. See here Thomas Aquinas on the vice of false humility, in *Summa Theologica* II-II.161.1 ad 2.

17. Bonhoeffer, *Life Together*, 95.

community: Christ's mediation alone. By the same coin, my gifts—unreceived and unheard—should be put to work elsewhere, in the days apart, in work, in ministry beyond the body, in the hopes that they will be cultivated in their exercise and find ground in which to bear fruit.

Such slights are frequent in church, though. But here too, meekness—our common entrance into Christ's body by forgiveness—comes to our aid. Writing in an almost masochistic manner, Bonhoeffer says, "My sin is of necessity the worst, the most serious, the most objectionable. . . . Those who would serve others in the community must descend all the way down to these depths of humility."[18] Bonhoeffer's identifying himself as, like the apostle Paul, "the chief of sinners" sounds like rhetorical excess here.[19] But by this, Bonhoeffer means to show that one's self-evaluation is *not* conditioned by comparison with others, which simply invites one back into viewing church as a struggle between strong and weak. If I approach the wrongs of others with a presumptive sense that my sin, as I view it, is less pervasive than that of others and that my fellow Christian is lower because of this evaluation, I have not only created a new measure by which she and I are joined together that favors me but also placed myself once again at the center of community, as the arbiter of how a community works.

The emphasis on meekness is in the end not only about true estimation of one's sins but about one's gifts. To exercise meekness is to reposition our relationship to others by affirming Christ's promises of pardon above all else and affirming Christ's promise that you are a person, irrespective of your gifts exercised. If we are joined together only by Christ, then when I look at others—including my enemy in the church—I see Christ first, our union, and thus must pass through Christ's gracious judgment of others en route to speaking any words, offering my gifts, proffering my experience and wisdom. This kind of meekness does not require jettisoning any kind of moral

18. Bonhoeffer, *Life Together*, 97–98.
19. See further Peter C. Bouteneff, "'I Am the Foremost of Sinners' (1 Tim 1:15): Negotiating the Church's Language of Self-Condemnation," in *Repentance and Forgiveness*, ed. Matthew E. Burdette and Victor Lee Austin (Eugene, OR: Cascade Books, 2020), 73–83.

evaluation—calling good evil or evil good—or dismissing what actual gifts we have to give, but it requires us to speak to even those who wrong us by first passing through Christ's evaluation of them. We cannot call them first anything other than what Christ has called them: a forgiven sinner.

Putting on Habits of Christian Community

Our bodily habits of community, proceeding along the lines of speech and exchange, require us to begin by "putting off" certain pathological ways of life—and so we begin with being slow to speak and slow to judge the ways in which a community receives the gifts I want to bring it. But it is not enough to simply avoid the ways of Adam and equate this with being Christian. Abstention from a vice is not the same as cultivating a virtue. Likewise, clearing space for community by meekness and silence is just the *precursor* for better speech to emerge. As Oliver O'Donovan has rightly argued, communication is the basis for community, both political and ecclesial; we are a creation that was summoned into being by the Word, to respond in the agency given us—we can only clear ground so long before we have to speak.[20]

The silence that precedes our speaking is not to be understood as piously trying to move beyond language but as disciplining the roar of idle talk. But silence and speech belong together, as do the purging of vice and the putting on of virtue. At some point, the habits by which we approach others—the things we put off and avoid—must be paired with positive practices if the deep roots of isolation are to be replaced by the fruit of knowing Christ in community. All else is simply deferring speech, by which the Word of God approaches us and binds us together.

Listening: The Entrance to Union

Because all communities are composed of not just the physically and economically but the *spiritually* strong and weak, some speaking

20. Oliver O'Donovan, *Ethics as Theology*, vol. 2, *Finding and Seeking* (Grand Rapids: Eerdmans, 2014), 12.

of God will be true to Scripture, some will be analogical speech that requires testing, and some will be heretical, however intended.

This is different than recognizing the dignity of all persons: it is the acknowledgment that, in a body that is diversely given, not each thought or spoken word is to be valued as equal to every other. To put off *all* speaking out of concerns for meekness can lead us astray here. For the way in which we offer contributions to the community—the way we speak and the way we listen here—corresponds to the way Christ approaches us.[21]

The asymmetry of the analogy is important: just as God is not the same as humans but in Christ joins with humanity so that we might be changed, so our hearing the words of God and our receiving the words of others are not the same. We do not receive all words by listening so that they might be put on par with the spoken promises of Scripture. The listening that God does is inseparable—but distinct— from the speech of God, and so it is then with the community of Christ: our anxieties, expositions, and wisdom are all taken up into the community, but they are not the foundation of the community. Our words illuminate, illustrate, and press for more words to be given, and as we engage, our words, thoughts, and wisdom are transformed, chastened, and raised up.

When we listen, we give occasion for words of wisdom to come up through the gathered bodies of the church;[22] listening offers all persons, not only the ordained, to contribute to this dynamic of purification and inclusion. It is by listening that the Christian, as a speaker of the Word, is offered not only the discipline of putting off "prattle in the presence of God" but also the opportunity to cultivate pastoral care. In a culture of isolation, we establish our place in the world by making ourselves known, by staking our claim and standing on our opinions and words. The discipline of listening thus gives the listener the opportunity of having their words purified by the words

21. Bonhoeffer, *Life Together*, 98: "God's love for us is shown by the fact that God not only gives us God's Word but also lends us God's ear."

22. "A Christian community does not consist solely of preachers of the Word" (Bonhoeffer, *Life Together*, 98). This insight remains particularly important for undoing the gendered presumptions surrounding what counts as wisdom in church speech. See Letty Russell, *Church in the Round: Feminist Interpretation of the Church* (Louisville: Westminster John Knox, 1993).

of a member of the body and opens the speaker to being included in the community as well. The disagreements and arguments—which may be significant and strong—are signs not of power in this frame but of dignity: disagreement and discourse occur when speakers are regarded as speakers bringing gifts that must be taken seriously.

This finds its analogue in Christ's action: by listening to us—attending to us—God includes us, so that we might share in the work of God. In listening (attending to the words being spoken, asking clarifying questions, and doing more than simply refraining from speaking) we learn how to distinguish between the prattle of our speaking (words of self-justification, of staking our place) and that which is true speech, words of building up, of reflecting the Scriptures, of holiness. And if *speech* is the way we have access to one another, then the truer our speech becomes, the more our community reflects the Word who gives us to be bearers of words. In listening, we are anticipating and attending: we do not know what God or the speaker will do, so we remain in communion by paying attention, responding, centering them in our attention instead of simply waiting to offer our words.

The oft-maligned practices of testimony in church belong here, as do the more onerous practices of parliamentary procedure in church discussions: the silence given to a speaker is the time in which they can make their offering and in which the hearer can attend to their communication. In listening, we receive the other person and so put aside both our own isolation (which simply wants to overcome the other person with our own explanations or words) and their isolation (which speaks in search of someone to respond). For what we receive from God centers and disciplines our own speech; likewise, listening and receiving the words from another before speaking disciplines our dreams about what the Christian community should be and learns to receive what God is doing in our midst.

Neighborliness: The Death of Our Individual Plans

If the first habit is that of listening—to make space for the words of another to flourish before God, so that our speech together might be elevated by the work of Christ—action and assistance of the speaker follows from this, responding to that which we have heard. To pair these motions together—hearing and action—is the character of discipleship, such that in the community of Christ, these two motions cannot be separated: as Bonhoeffer famously remarked, "Only the believers obey, and only the obedient believe."[23] Listening and action, by analogy to "obeying and believing," do not exist as chronologically sequential: in some cases we listen and then meet the need, and sometimes we create the condition in which the ones who cannot be heard can speak. There are times when the response is a declining of the words spoken, but again, this is not as a pure refusal but as an invitation to community: in Matthew (18:15–18), when the one in sin refuses to repent, the response is more speech, with the restoration of the community in view.[24]

To name the fellow Christian as "the neighbor" strikes us as odd, in that we associate neighbor with "stranger." But naming all others than myself as the "neighbor" is where we must begin—all who are not ourselves are, in the view of the two great commandments, neighbors, even if they are our own families.[25] The love that is due to the ones we listen to is due to them as the neighbor to whom we listen and then respond. As we saw in chapter 3, to say that there are some who are *not* neighbors here is to say that there is a relationship that does not need Christ's repair, which is to consign that beloved relationship to the fields of isolation.

If the ones we listen to are not intimates, theologically speaking, but neighbors, then we hear them (rightly) in some ways as strangers who deserve our attention to hear well. It is not enough, in other words, to listen in a way that already anticipates their answer; rather, we must listen in a way that seeks to understand, to ask clarifying

23. Dietrich Bonhoeffer, *Discipleship*, trans. Barbara Green and Reinhard Krauss, Dietrich Bonhoeffer Works 4 (Minneapolis: Fortress, 2001), 65.

24. Here, even the one being confronted does not repent; they remain "as a tax collector," which is to say one whom Jesus has called, one who has not *yet* responded but who may later respond—as is repeatedly the case in Jesus's parables.

25. Consider that in the form of the commandment found in Leviticus, the command "You shall love your neighbor as yourself" (Lev. 19:18) is preceded by "You shall not hate in your heart anyone of your kin; you shall reprove your neighbor" (19:17). So "neighbor" seems to be equated with "brother/kin." I am indebted to copyeditor Robert Banning for pointing me to this.

questions, and to invite in with our actions. The good Samaritan provides the model for Bonhoeffer here: "We must be ready to allow ourselves to be interrupted by God, who will thwart our plans and frustrate our ways time and again, even daily, by sending people across our path with their demands and requests. We can, then, pass them by, preoccupied with our more important daily tasks, just as the priest—perhaps reading the Bible—passed by the man who had fallen among robbers."[26]

The parable of the good Samaritan has a long and storied history of interpretation, read variously from Augustine to Margaret Thatcher.[27] But what we find in this reading is that the church-community is not only to put that which is heard into practice but also to be in search of those who need the listening, elevation of speech, and aid that cannot be had apart from the community. The Samaritan and the man beaten on the road exist as those on the edges of the story: the Samaritan because of his ethnicity and the beaten man because of the damage done to him and because of his namelessness. But it is precisely these two—the socially "weak"—who model for the parable's hearers what it means to join care for others with the love of God.

Consider, for example, what this means for social ministry. In the last fifty years, a sea change has occurred within Christian social ministry from models that emphasized emergency aid to ones that emphasize capacity building. The impetus here was to minimize paternalistic arrangements, whereby the poor were continuously dependent on the well-off, to free the poor by giving them not just temporary aid but skills.[28] But despite the strides forward in terms

26. Bonhoeffer, *Life Together*, 99.

27. Nick Spencer, *The Political Samaritan: How Power Hijacked a Parable* (London: Bloomsbury, 2018); Riemer Roukema, "The Good Samaritan in Ancient Christianity," *Vigiliae Christianae* 58 (2004): 56–74.

28. Key directions in this conversation can be found in Steve Corbett and Brian Fikkert, *When Helping Hurts: How to Alleviate Poverty without Hurting the Poor . . . and Yourself* (Chicago: Moody, 2009); Robert Lupton, *Toxic Charity: How Churches and Charities Hurt Those They Help (And How to Reverse It)* (New York: HarperOne, 2011); Dambisa Moyo, *Dead Aid: Why Aid Is Not Working and How There Is a Better Way for Africa* (New York: Farrar, Straus & Giroux, 2010); and Daniel G. Groody, ed., *The Option for the Poor in Christian Theology* (Notre Dame, IN: University of Notre Dame Press, 2010).

of what it means to love one's neighbor—shifting from paternalism
to capacity building, honoring the dignity of the one in need—this
new model still turns on an anthropology that takes isolation and
separation as the baseline, for even in this model, we must be free to
make our choices apart from one another to be fully human.

But what if the love given to the neighbors refuses the terms of
isolation, extending the internal goods of the church-community into
this space of helping and aiding? Theologically, what is needed by
people is not only to have their needs met but to have them met in a
manner that undoes *isolation* as well as giving in a way that recognizes
my isolation from the one I give to. The way forward here cannot
simply be to send a person out so that they can autonomously build
their own life or to respond to needs in a way that turns the neighbor
back toward their own resources and answers: capacity-building and
asset-based benevolence is better than paternalist charity, but it still
assumes autonomy as a feature of its framework. Thoroughgoing
helpfulness—to love them as a neighbor—means not only incorporating them into the community, where they are freed to be persons
in community, joined with the lives of others, but also treating their
presence as God's work: they are joined to me in Christ and not an
extension of myself, and I am in need of their presence as the bearer
of God's work.

The ministry of being a neighbor—whether with respect to those
present or to those who need to be included yet—continues the negative work of meekness by putting it into positive form. We withdraw
ourselves and our desire to overcome others in order to replace our
self-assertion with a practice by which we continually invite others
into the heart of our deliberations: how to spend our days and our
common resources, and how to build our common life. In this way,
Jesus's statement that "the poor you will always have among you"
is an invitation to be among the poor in such a way that their gifts,
leadership, and agency are those gifts without which the church cannot be the church, and in such a way that they are those whom the
church aids not only by its relief but also by its communion. As Jean
Daniélou reminds us, we do not love so that a person does what we
desire—that is, join the church—for our actions in this way are trying to overcome the distance between people by making them more

bourgeois.[29] We love others so that we and they might be healed together in Christ, and so that our common life might reflect that union, materially and spiritually.

Bearing One Another: Beyond "My" Sin or "Yours"

If, in the community of Christ, we are to be at one another's disposal, ordering our words and gifts, this takes us into a deeper theological space: bearing one another's guilt and sin. Here, aims and goals of the Christian with respect to sin must go beyond mere noninterference and venture into what it means that the congregation members bear one another as sinners: "The law of Christ is a law of forbearance."[30] Here, the language and action toward one another move into more dangerous territory, ordered beyond the notion that we only know one another in joy and celebration, and toward the notion that we know what shape the body of Christ takes in the world when sinners bear one another.

"Solidarity," the adopting of another person's struggle as one's own, is, as we discussed in chapter 1, a beginning point here, not the end. The union between persons in solidarity begins in the place of common struggle, of some deficiency or inequity that has emerged, with community occurring to address that. But the language of "vicarious suffering"—a theological bearing of the burdens of another—is built on the premise that the suffering of sin is part of the human condition: it does not come and go in waves, and so our communion with one another must pass beyond solidarity and into this place of being cobearers of one another's sin.[31]

Ephraim Radner, a contemporary Anglican theologian, points us to the difficulty of seeing this here: we have assumed, wrongly, that the work of the Spirit is to remove suffering and difficulty.[32] In the modern

29. Jean Daniélou, *Prayer as a Political Problem*, ed. and trans. Joseph Richard Kirwan (London: Burns and Oates, 1967), 6–8.

30. Bonhoeffer, *Life Together*, 100.

31. For a full treatment of this theme of vicarious representation, see Christine Schliesser, *Everyone Who Acts Responsibly Becomes Guilty: Bonhoeffer's Concept of Accepting Guilt* (Louisville: Westminster John Knox, 2008).

32. See particularly Ephraim Radner, *A Profound Ignorance: Modern Pneumatology and Its Anti-Modern Redemption* (Waco: Baylor University Press, 2019); and

era, Radner argues, we conflate ending suffering with the work of the Spirit, such that we have no way to make sense of sustained suffering or of why Christians should engage in the prolonged suffering (and by extension, the lingering sin) of others. The culprit here is a deficient anthropology, in which the human essence is not bound to creation in a way that would require lingering with the persistence of suffering and sin. This deficient vision of the human, as one who "truly" exists apart from the bonds of creation, is condemned to draw on its own resources for its spiritual and moral survival; if one struggles with sin, it is because of no fault other than one's own lack of will. For guilt and sin are incurred solely through individual hands and hearts, and thus remedied in the same isolated way. If a Christian is made alive by the Spirit, this model assumes, they have all they need, and my actions add nothing to this.

Scripture, however, promises no such thing, either with respect to the sufficiency of the individual or with respect to the removal of suffering as a feature of creaturely life. The Spirit-breathed community of Christ is not immune from or devoid of suffering, for in Christ's commission, the disciples are promised not only that they will be taken places they do not wish to go but also that in the end they will be *martyros*, martyrs-cum-witnesses. If it is the work of the Spirit to conform us to Christ, then the shape of our journey out of isolation into community (as we see in Acts) is tied up with suffering and with the persistent bearing of one another's burdens—to the point of bearing sin with one another.

But the suffering that we must keep in view is not just martyrdom and hardship but the burdens and *sins* of one another in the community.[33] If our union with each other is through Christ, then we are connected to one another solely through Christ's person and *in Christ's way*. We join with one another insofar as we also share with Christ's own suffering in our bearing of one another; as Paul writes, we *fill up Christ's own suffering* as we do this (Col. 1:24). This is

---

Radner, *A Brutal Unity: The Spiritual Politics of the Christian Church* (Waco: Baylor University Press, 2012).

33. Bonhoeffer, *Life Together*, 101: "[Christ] bore them as a mother carries her child, as a shepherd enfolds the lost lamb that has been found. . . . Christians share in this law."

simply the way in which the church participates in the person and work of Christ: by discipleship, entering into the way of Christ, which is bearing with others' burdens of sin and difficulty.

This concept of bearing one another's weakness comes under particular scrutiny in that it can be used paternalistically, from an assumption that the ones whose suffering is borne possess no agency. But this is to miss the salient point: it is not that the ones being borne have no agency but that others are called to add to the agency of the ones suffering in sin, and vice versa. This is where "bearing" goes beyond sympathy or pity: it is one thing for us to bear with the physical frailties or helplessness of another person, to visit the sick or sit with the dying, but it is another to bear with the *sin* of others—and the damage that attends it.

The spiritually strong here, as elsewhere, find a greater obligation given to them—to pray, intercede, and counsel—but also a special temptation: to hold their aid over the strong as a debt instead of elevating the weak. But the spiritually weak, too, must guard themselves, so that if they are aiding the strong, they do not take joy in the fall of the strong. The reversals of fortune in Scripture, the leveling of the valleys, are not for destruction but so that the Zacchaeuses might come down from the tree and the centurions might humble themselves to the son of Mary. All are joined together in one vision and vocation here, such that it is not simply in the interest of all to be faithful; rather, it is for the sake of Christ that all are to be borne with.

The analogy between Christ's own mediation for us and our mediation for others is not accidental. If the church mirrors in its discipleship what it sees with Christ, then this entails suffering for others not as an additional feature but as an act intrinsic to discipleship, including suffering that guilt that fellow church members incur as well as the guilt that our neighbors have.[34] If we are knit together into one body of Christ, then there can be no sense in which my guilt or sin does not affect your well-being, but likewise, I help to bear the

34. See Jennifer McBride's *The Church for the World: A Theology of Public Witness* (Oxford: Oxford University Press, 2012), 127–52, for the theological roots to this theme in Bonhoeffer, and see Guido de Graaff, "Intercession as Political Ministry: Re-interpreting the Priesthood of All Believers," *Modern Theology* 32 (2016): 504–21, for one provocative recasting of this theme in terms of church witness in the world.

consequences of your sin and work toward your redemption as part of our common calling in Christ. The Christian is not one who is afraid of the entangling effects of original sin, in which the world exists in a common state of fallenness, a state that present members did not cause, strictly speaking. We share this world in its fallen state, but for that reason, we also share this world in its salvation in Christ.[35]

For in bearing with one another in *sin*, we are acknowledging that there is truly nothing that can persist beyond the love of God. Even the one whom Paul writes of as being put out from the community remains *a part of the community*, ministered to so that they might be drawn back in. The sin of one affects all within the body, but this is all the more reason for the body to bear and forgive the fallen member, for in doing so, the body brings about that member's healing and becomes more like the Christ who centers and sustains it.

Proclamation: Calling One Another Home

If our life together is one of bearing sin, it is also one of breaking into the sin of others with words of pardon and return. Preaching—as one of the most prominent forms of diagnosing the sin we bear together and of proclaiming Christ's pardon—jumps first to our mind when we think about "proclamation." The Reformation emphasis on the preached Word is critical here, for we are joined together by Christ and in Christ, and it is in preaching that the Word approaches us. But our speech to one another in preaching arises from and returns to a common life, for we can only speak to one another about the things that we share, and what we share is a life in Christ. The Christian needs counsel, encouragement, wisdom, and instruction beyond the sermon. This proclamation, this ad hoc form of ministry, is the kind that emerges in the folds of a life together and is different from preaching, and so emerges within context, generated by our times of reading, prayer, eating, and worship: our lives together form the shared context of trust into which we can speak the truths of the Scripture to one another in a way that is not "empty talk."[36]

35. "For since death came through a human being, the resurrection of the dead has also come through a human being; for as all die in Adam, so all will be made alive in Christ" (1 Cor. 15:21–22).

36. Bonhoeffer, *Life Together*, 104.

There is a real danger to the way in which Scripture enters into our common life, a danger both of neglecting to speak it when it is the word that needs to be spoken (thus abandoning each person to their own resources) and speaking it to excess (thus diminishing the person as one who is not an equal). For to speak it too much risks talking away real needs, offering Scripture as a dismissal for the concrete pains and difficulties of one's fellow member. Using Scripture in this way treats Scripture as if it were an abstraction, a "timeless truth" that stands over against time, whereas Scripture is the Word of God, the vehicle for God's address to us in this time and this place. Scripture is deeply knit into our lives, not an objective lever over them, for Christ is among us, not beyond us.

This is the danger of such ad hoc proclamation, that when we speak Scripture to one another, we do so either in ways that dominate them or in ways that refuse to see the Scriptures as reflecting a Word who is heard by us in time. But it is also the freedom of this kind of speech that the community has not only the ability but the *responsibility* to speak to one another in ways that allow us to be one another's keepers. This can be done badly, in ways that conform the other person to our image (replicating the logic of the crowd in miniature).[37] But as we have seen, if speech is the way in which we have access to one another, speech that is centered in Christ is the vehicle by which we call one another back to our common home. This speech is "a service of mercy, the ultimate offer of genuine community";[38] it is only when our sin is named as such, even when our own judgment dismisses the words of another, that we can return to Christ and thus to one another.[39] When it is Scripture that is spoken, with Christ our center, the judgment intrinsic to the word spoken falls both on the

37. See chap. 2.

38. Bonhoeffer, *Life Together*, 105.

39. "Judgment" here is used in the ordinary form of the term, the act of making a judgment about what is to be said or done, not the legal form of rendering judgment as representatives of the law. We cannot live or speak without making judgments about what should be done or said in this circumstance. To avoid making judgments for fear of seeming *judgmental* is to never speak or act, to remain in the position of the third servant of the talents (Matt. 25:14–30), afraid of doing the wrong thing and so doing the wrong thing by risking no actions or words. On this topic of ordinary judgment and its political ramifications, see Oliver O'Donovan, *The Ways of Judgment* (Grand Rapids: Eerdmans, 2003), 7–13.

one who is addressed *and* on the speaker, calling both to account and both to Christ. In speaking words of judgment, the speaker does not seek to break off fellowship but to draw the addressee out of hiding and back into the community.

The kind of proclamation we offer corresponds to the nature of authority that the Christian church has, Rowan Williams argues. The authority of the Christian is tied into its credibility: the church remains authoritative in its speech and proclamation to the degree that it has committed itself to the way of Christ together.[40] In this way, the members of Christ's body share in this mutual authority to pardon us and promise Christ's grace to us, and our public credibility—our authority as sharers of the message—is tied into our language being chastened by our penitence, particularly when we bring the Scriptures to bear on the intimate places of our common life. There is no way in which our bearing with one another is allowed to be placed in a subsidiary place to authority, for we are the body of Christ insofar as we receive Christ's presence among us again and again, remaining on the way with Christ in the power of the Spirit.

Authority: Holding the Body's Shape

But how does this body hold together? How does it resolve disputes, name its norms? Here, let us hazard a different kind of habit from the ones above: that of authorizing and leading. Authority in the Christian world has come on hard times, not exclusively due to the abuses that can come from spiritual authority but also because of the divorce between authority and the authenticity of the one in authority. Authority does not, as such, self-authenticate, and one is not authoritative in the life of the body merely because one has been ordained. Rather, authority is borne out and *dependent on* the marks of the community named above: "Jesus tied all authority in the community to service, one to another. . . . The longing we so often hear expressed today for 'episcopal figures,' 'priestly people,' 'authoritative personalities' often enough stems from a spiritually sick need to admire human beings and to establish visible human

40. Rowan Williams, "The Authority of the Church," *Modern Believing* 46 (2005): 16–28.

authority because the genuine authority of service appears to be too insignificant."[41]

Authority is inseparable from questions of those who embody Christian faithfulness, gifted by the Spirit, who have been shaped by the practices of the life together and called out by Christ from among the congregation. In descriptions of authority throughout church history, it is the *assumption* that the minister embodies these things: when one looks at the qualifications of the bishop in 1 Timothy 3, for example, it appears that the leader of the church is one from among the body, not one who comes to the church as an administrative authority. Benedict of Nursia, when describing the abbot, the one who is to be obeyed within the community by the monks, likewise characterizes him as one who first "points out to them all that is good and holy more by example than by words."[42]

Spiritual authority frequently emerges in various ways and often from those spaces occupied by, in the language of Paul, despised members of the body, shaming the powerful and wise of the world (1 Cor. 1:28). Whether the community can recognize the authority of these saints when it appears depends on whether it is looking for those who have been formed in this way or whether it is looking for those who have administrative acumen. This is not to dismiss the need for ministers who have been adequately trained over time—indeed, the assumption that ministers need only the direct instruction of the Spirit is an ironically modern invention.

In the community, it is not the case that authority is a vacated concept, desacralized as a form of management theory: because the community is of the Spirit, the representative authority remains of the people, shepherding them in their language, prayer, reading, and discipleship. To have *no* authority is to designate each individual an authority over their fragment of the world. But there likewise is a hollow form of authority that is alien to the community of faith: the pure administrator who refuses to be equal to the people.[43] Pastoral authority in the body of Christ is a charism, a gifting that is

41. Bonhoeffer, *Life Together*, 106.

42. Benedict of Nursia, *The Rule of Benedict*, ed. Timothy Fry, OSB (New York: Vintage, 1981), 9.

43. Bonhoeffer, *Life Together*, 107.

cultivated from within and comes not for the sake of reinstating a divide between laity and the ordained but for the sake of cultivating the discipleship of all.[44] For the one who is recognized by the community as having authority is the one who is most shaped in the ways of meekness, humility, silence, helpfulness, and the like: the ones content to be disciples of Jesus and to be dispossessive of their own sense of calling that does not cultivate the community's life and witness. To quote William Stringfellow, the lay Episcopalian theologian, "Within the polity of the church it is a facet of fidelity to the gospel to remember that everyone remains baptized, everyone participates in the ministry of the laity, everyone has the status of servant. Those who are ecclesiastically ordered, as deacons or priests or bishops or those who enter upon the monastic life, do not thereby surrender or alter or diminish their disposition as laity, as baptized people, as members of the body of Christ called to the world's service."[45]

The minister who is *not* truly a part of the community is the one who feels their authority challenged by a word of admonition by a congregant and thus facilitates the isolation of sin and amplifies it by their status within the community. Ministers trained in seminaries, whether in Phuket or Finkenwalde or Abilene or Nairobi, would certainly learn methods for scriptural interpretation, the practice and theory of ministry, church history, theological confessions, and more. These elements of a minister's training are in some real ways the training of a specialist: pastoral care, homiletics, and moral theology are not intuitive skills but require practice and time. But the training of the minister is part of a complex toolkit that now can permeate and aid—not subvert—the core disciplines of the church's shared life.

In their recent treatment of ministerial failure, Scot McKnight and Laura Barringer point toward a vision of pastoral authority that is charged with cultivating a church culture of openness, transparency,

44. William Stringfellow, *A Keeper of the Word: Selected Writings of William Stringfellow*, ed. Bill Kellerman (Grand Rapids: Eerdmans, 1994), 165: "For those ordained by the church for the priesthood, this means that their office and ministry are located at the interstices of the body of Christ and of the congregations that represent the Body visibly and notoriously in the world. The ministry of the priesthood is a ministry to the members of the Body in their relations to each other, relations consequent to their incredibly diversified ministry within the world."

45. Stringfellow, *Keeper of the Word*, 162.

and mutual care. At the heart here is the conviction that the church reflects the divine intention for creation—goodness, or *tov*, the word spoken by God over creation.[46] Pastoral abuse emerges precisely in the place where the minister finds themselves separate from the congregation and thus indulging in the isolation of sin—separate and competing with the church over what God's vision of the church is. It is in this spirit that we see authority as a practice of ministerial wisdom: the minister has been called together with this people, not in a form of authority that dictates, but in a form that models, embodies, and persuades.

Conclusion: On Ministry and Mission

The shape of ministry—and in particular the contour of negative and positive disciplines—highlights the ways in which the center of the Christian community is that which grows from the ground up. It is a community that emerges not according to a recognized order so much as according to a recognizable pattern of character: that of Jesus Christ. As the Spirit draws the community together, it takes the shape of Christ in the world, as its ministry is ordered toward the building of the community; as the community gathers and scatters, it remains the image of Christ, learning from all of the goods of creation and taking them into the community so that all of creation might be hallowed by Christ.

This kind of community has an integral nature, for it not only seeks to be grounded in the world God has placed it in but also knits together that which is fractured: church from world, person from person, minister from congregant. This knitting together is a matter of habit and time, and it is precisely this fabric of reality, made up of habit and time, that is sustained by none other than the Christ whom we meet in worship. The Christian community need feel no rush to find its place in the world, for in pursuing the life of the community, the concerns and fragments of the world are already within

46. Scot McKnight and Laura Barringer, *A Church Called Tov: Forming a Goodness Culture That Resists Abuses of Power and Promotes Healing* (Carol Stream, IL: Tyndale Momentum, 2020), 88–91.

it: by being a neighbor to the world within the church-community, it has the basis on which to care for that which is already writ large throughout creation.[47]

For the church-community that is seeking to bear the burdens of others, to be a neighbor, to listen, and to speak—as it grows in these habits—will yearn to practice these habits not only in the day together but also in the many days apart. And so, what first we might view (and loathe) as the expanded kingdom of isolation (the many days of separation) becomes the occasion for isolation to be permeated by the kingdom of God. We must only pay attention, expecting that indeed the Spirit is always drawing us deeper into sharing the sufferings of Christ and that we will be sustained by the risen Christ in the going.

47. To reiterate an earlier point, this is why we have emphasized the practices and habits of the Christian life instead of narrating first according to principles: a principle such as "advocacy for life," while providing summary guidance for the Christian life, gives us no overt indicators as to what life is, how it is to be advocated for, or in what priority. But beginning with attending to the specifics of the lives among the church-community—the ways in which bodily lives are impinged on, afflicted, empowered, and burdened—churches have the basis for being able to advocate more specifically and in a more nuanced fashion: they have learned first on the basis of the goods that God has placed among them to learn the habits of attention necessary to reach out more broadly. Principles are rational summaries, from this perspective, of concerns that emerge as we attend to God's act in the gathering and gifting of Christ's body within the scope of creation's redemption.

Seven

Life Together Made Visible

CONFESSION AND COMMUNION

As we saw in chapter 3, Christ is the one who draws us together and is present among us, and as we engage in the practices of the church-community, we are being healed of the deep poison of isolation, the sign of sin. It is not enough for one to merely enter into the community, any more than it is sufficient to go to the doctor to get a prescription for an illness. For in the same way that we go to the doctor in order to become well, so that we might live more fully, so we engage in the practices of silence, listening, and helping so that we might live more fully as the body of Christ. And so now we approach the practices that the others have been preparing us for and that enable the others: confession and forgiveness. These practices invite us to see the face of another and enter into communion with them.

Sin as Isolation: The Loss of Confession

In the sixteenth century, the Christian church was divided again as the Reformers in Europe—Martin Luther, John Calvin, Thomas Cranmer, and others—refused the authority of Rome and continued to be

Christian apart from it.[1] The reasons for this are complex, and the Reformers' intentions are complicated, and these will not concern us here. But in their various reforms, they distinguished practices that were essential to the faith from those that were not, and they gave reasons. Luther in particular believed that there were many things that Christians—Roman Catholic and not—shared and that there was no reason to abandon: Why would one abandon forms of corporate prayer or practices of reading Scripture that encouraged you to preach through the whole Bible?

But one of the practices that fell into disrepair across time was the discipline of confession.[2] In the Roman Catholic Church, the priest stands in for the person of Christ, not as Christ incarnate but in a way similar to how Christ represents the church before God the Father.[3] As the priest mediates the words, power, and authority of Christ to the gathered body, as the representative of Christ to the people, the people are assured that their confession and prayers are heard and received by Christ. What this means with respect to confession is that for Christians, confession is done to the one who has the representative power, in the name of Jesus, to tell the people that their sins are forgiven. The priest, as Christ's representative, reminds the confessing Christian that Christ is greater than their sin, and the priest administers to the Christian certain tasks appropriate to do in light of their forgiveness (penance).

1. Centuries prior to the sixteenth-century Reformations, delegations of Pope Leo IX and Patriarch Michael I Cerularius of Constantinople issued mutual anathemas in 1054, the culmination of centuries of division and the inauguration of new hostilities in the twelfth and thirteenth centuries. In other words, the break between Luther and the Catholic Church of the sixteenth century was not the first breach of Christ's body to emerge but continued in the wake of earlier breaches and the consolidations in the centuries that followed. See Henry Chadwick, *East and West: The Making of a Rift in the Church: From Apostolic Times until the Council of Florence* (Oxford: Oxford University Press, 2003).

2. For an overview of the diversity of confessional practices during this period, see Katharine Jackson Lualdi and Anne T. Thayer, eds., *Penitence in the Age of Reformations* (Aldershot, UK: Ashgate, 2000).

3. This configuration appears in Thomas Aquinas's *Summa Theologica* III.78.1 with reference to the Eucharist: "But the form of this sacrament is pronounced as if Christ were speaking in person, so that it is given to be understood that the minister does nothing in perfecting this sacrament, except to pronounce the words of Christ."

Luther abandoned penance in particular, not because Christians do not need to confess their sins but because he thought that holding the priest as Christ's mediating representative in this fashion was an error. But although he did not think that Christians need to offer confession of their sin to a priest any longer, he did not think that that meant confession of sin *to other people* is either wrong or unnecessary. Rather, Luther decentralized the practice: because we are the gathered body of Christ, confession can be offered by any Christian to any Christian, with one condition: when we offer confession, we are to remind one another that Christ has forgiven us of our sin. We are to preach gospel to our fellow Christians, not law—we know too well why we are confessing, and in our despair concerning our sin we need to hear that Christ has forgiven us fully.[4]

Over time, however, this practice, too, gradually became lost, as confession of sin *to each other* became confession of sin *only to God.* The reasoning behind this development was that sin is ultimately against God, for all sin—even the most heinous sins against our neighbors—is a sin against the God who has made our neighbors. So if sin is ultimately a sin against God, no matter what form it appears in, why do I need to confess it to *other people*? Why should I tell someone else about a sin committed that directly affects them in no way?[5]

Confession to a fellow Christian is important for two reasons. First, as we have seen, sin is never privatized, any more than the spiritual growth or virtue of the Christian is a singular work: sin and its effects never remain with us; thus, bearing that sin is not the work that a Christian is ever called to do alone. When I become a morally vicious person—when I am greedy or lustful or angry—it affects the community in all kinds of ways, small and large. And so, when I sin,

4. Though Luther holds to penance in the opening of his *Babylonian Captivity of the Church*, he rejects it by the end of the work. On Luther's view of why confession is a more appropriate model than penance for the confession of sin, see Ronald K. Rittgers, "Penance, Confession, Forgiveness, and Reconciliation in Martin Luther's Context and Writings," *Oxford Research Encyclopedia of Religion*, March 29, 2017, https://doi.org/10.1093/acrefore/9780199340378.013.361.

5. On the historical decline of confession in the post-Reformation world, see Annemarie S. Kidder, *Making Confession, Hearing Confession: A History of the Cure of Souls* (Collegeville, MN: Liturgical Press, 2010), 230–42.

I am depriving another Christian of the full gift of the community of the body of Christ, and I need to confess that, hearing the pardon of Christ through the mouth of another.

But second, when I do not confess to another person, I am perpetuating the isolation of sin for *religious* reasons: I am withdrawing from others and hiding from them the sin that is affecting them, claiming that I need only confess to God. I am withdrawing from both the reckoning that must occur and from the pardon that will be offered, whereas the work of Christ, we have seen, comes to us always from the outside, through the faces and mouths of the body of Christ.

What I need—the forgiveness of Christ, the promises of God, reconciliation with Christ's body—comes as I seek communion with Christ's body. When we lose the capacity to confess to one another, it is in part because we do not see that it is through the gathered body that Christ comes to us or that, indeed, the church *is* Christ's body, wounded and historically distended as it is. When confession is rendered a private activity, that is an indicator that we do not see the frail, fragile, limping church as Christ's own body. Apart from confession, we can always disavow the broken body of Christ that we belong to in favor of some idealized community that has never existed. And in doing so, we dismiss not only the work that God is already doing among us but also the mission of the one who took on flesh so that creation might be redeemed.

The End and New Beginning of Our Life Together

It is here that we see why discussion of this practice is saved for last. Before we can confess our sins to one another—as the culminating practice of the Christian life—we must first learn how to join with one another, how to entrust our prayers and our helping and our reading of Scripture to another. It is far more humbling to stand before someone to ask for forgiveness than it is to help them: in helping, I can render aid with a hidden sense of superiority, holding myself apart from them even in my aid. But in asking for forgiveness, I leave all pretense behind and stand before another person with nothing but need. And what do I need more than reconciliation with Christ's own body?[6]

The incarnation sets the conditions for what the church is: the church is Christ's body, and, as Irenaeus reminded us, Christ became what we are that we might become like Christ. But scandalously, Christ—and thus, Christ's body—is marked not by strength but by weakness, meekness, silence, borrowed words offered as those of God. If we trust the Christ who called a body together, then we must trust those of the church to hear our confession and speak the words of Christ back to us. Confession becomes the breakthrough to our life together: through confession, we encounter one another, with Christ mediating our relationship.

But if confession is the culmination of our life together, then in another way, confession also leads us back out to the previously discussed practices. Envision here the Möbius strip, that paradoxical shape in which the loop has no beginning or end. For in the same way that confession is made possible by the trust that is learned through the other practices, so confession now enables the other practices more fully. As I confess and humble myself before others, I am able to set myself aside to let another read the Scriptures, to hear the pardoning words of one who in another setting would not be my social equal, to consider the insights of one who over a long life has learned the ways of Christ that have become unfashionable. Confession sends me back out of the church and into the world in humility and service, in reception and openness and the knowledge that my sins have been forgiven and that others are not threats to my standing before God, but gifts.

Confession and the Church's Mission

It may very well be that, for all of our gathering—for all of our learning how to be one body in eating, singing, and ministry—we are still just a crowd. For if the reason we gather together is to perform

6. See Stephen Westerholm, "Repentance and Forgiveness: Biblical Foundations," in *Repentance and Forgiveness*, ed. Matthew E. Burdette and Victor Lee Austin (Eugene, OR: Cascade Books, 2020), 1–20, for the contours of this argument.

certain activities, with others incidental celebrants alongside us, we have not touched the isolation that the church participates in and amplifies.[7] If, when we gather, we bring only our confessions of faith and not our confessions of sin, we are still gathering only as a crowd. Without the common confession of faith, we are only a body who knows how to judge in a way that divides, but without confession of sin, we are not a body that is willing to be healed.

This is one of the most difficult elements of the life together, particularly for questions of the church's mission, for the message that we are a gathered group of *sinners* is hardly attractive to a culture well aware of the church's limitations. But without this—without confession—we are under the illusion that what we are doing in gathering is creating a pure body. And when the purity of the body's practice is the constant preoccupation, our scrupulousness never ends, and we forget that for us as creatures, the watchword is *penitence* and not *perfection*.

Like the work of the day apart, confession takes on a missionary cast, for the words that are directed outward to the world take many forms. Sometimes, the words that are turned outward to the world are those of direct challenge, as with the sermon or the public statement; sometimes, the word turned outward is one of lament and consolation. The words that we habitually speak among ourselves, as we have seen, are those that we can speak well among others, bearing witness to the work of God among us. But the word of confession, too, has its place, for when we exercise it habitually among ourselves, it too can be turned outward.

Here, I do not mean "confession" in the sense of evangelism, but confession in the sense of affirming that our public acknowledgments have come up short. For some places, particularly those that can now be described as culturally "post-Christian," this is an acknowledgment painfully drawn out of them by their neighbors who

7. Dietrich Bonhoeffer, *Life Together*, trans. Daniel W. Bloesch, in *Life Together; Prayerbook of the Bible*, Dietrich Bonhoeffer Works 5 (Minneapolis: Fortress, 1996), 110: "Sin wants to be alone with people. It takes them away from the community. . . . Sin wants to remain unknown. It shuns the light. In the darkness of what is left unsaid sin poisons the whole being of a person." As we have noted before, language of "loneliness" indicates the symptoms of the deeper condition of isolation, not the fullness of the problem.

have long-suffered both the gifts and presumptions of Christians. But for those still living in a Christianized society, where prayers occur before city council meetings and at sporting events, confession as I have been describing it plays its part too. For if Christians bear witness to what Christ does among us, then that witness must take the shape of confession as much as it takes the form of proclamation.[8]

There are plenty of pious congregations who think themselves in no need of confession to the world, but public confession that we are sinners is what enables the proclamation: that *Christ* is among us, healing us, taking up our mortal frames, and in doing so, transforming the world. When the church refuses to enact confession among its own members, it risks not imaging the gospel to the world beyond the church. The church becomes that body whose members cannot bear one another's sin and cannot bear weakness, and will still persist in the world, but under the sign of the Pharisee and not of the publican. For gatherings held together only by a common experience, the act of confession deflates this, slows us down, poses questions to our practices; it runs counterproductively to a gathering that is purely celebratory. But this itself is revelatory: if our gathering cannot bear weakness, then it cannot bear Christ, the one who was made weak for us.

Confession: The New Starting Point

Confession, as a practice of the Christian community together, is the property of all persons. If we are in this together, then we can make and hear confession before another from among the baptized, irrespective of clerical status.[9] Confession is not therapy, the time to get something off your chest; if this were the case, then only certain persons with professional expertise would be the appropriate hearers. Rather, confession is the act that all persons of the church do together, regardless of our familiarity with the one who is confessing. For as we have seen, what binds even the most intimate of relationships

8. See Jeremy M. Bergen's *Ecclesial Repentance: The Churches Confront Their Sinful Pasts* (Edinburgh: T&T Clark, 2011) for an argument and historic examples of how the internal penitence of the church relates to its external confessions of wrongdoing and sinfulness.

9. Bonhoeffer, *Life Together*, 114.

together is nothing less than Christ's mediation; therefore, confession is dependent not on prior knowledge but on the common experience of being Christ's people.

This should be shared by all members, but not because of the most straightforward reason—namely, that confession is a shared burden of the church. To be sure, the carrying of the sins of others should not be a burden of only a few, but the shared responsibility of all members. But hearing a confession is a gift, for in it we are invited to be Christ's emissary, to offer the words of forgiveness, and to be entrusted with the depths of another person—and this gift should not be hoarded by a few![10]

The distance between contemplating confessing to my spouse and contemplating confessing to a stranger is, appropriately, a large one; with my spouse, I know that we share a history and understanding that not only couch the things confessed but also that will temper the response. But it is precisely this generous reception rooted in a common history that we are to be wary of, for it fosters the notion that the church is built ultimately on shared histories, common understandings, inside jokes. The risk of church is trusting that what we have in common is Christ and that if that is true, *anyone* can be of the church, from Pharisees to publicans. Everyone in Christ needs pardon, and so anyone can give and receive it in Christ.

For confession to be the "breakthrough" to Christian community, as Bonhoeffer describes it, confession must be done as we see in the image of the publican: *without* pretense and *with* specificity. In Protestant circles, it is common to speak of all sins as being equal, but this is truthful to the point of being dangerously banal. To be a sinner is to be a sinner both generally and specifically: we are all caught up in the condition of sin that pervades creation, but we are caught up in it *in specific ways*. If we, against the risk of confession, pull back from specificity and fall back on the first generic sense (that all are sinners), we not only misunderstand the nature of sin but also are using that sense of sin as another crowd to hide in. In

10. Bonhoeffer, *Life Together*, 116: "It is not a good thing for one person to be the confessor for all the others. All too easily this individual will become overburdened, one for whom confession becomes an empty routine, giving rise to the unholy misuse of confession for the exercise of spiritual tyranny over souls."

sinning *specifically*, we have made ourselves individuals, in that it is I who have done this sin, not another. And it is in that fracture that Christ wants to speak to draw me *as me* back into the community. The word to Peter was not that he was a generalized sinner forgiven of a concept of sin but that he was a traitor forgiven of betrayal, given the keys to the kingdom for all those who would think their own betrayals of Christ too deep to bear.

In starting anew, and starting from this *specific* vantage point, we see that our practices of community to this point have been preparation in trust and in community: we have been learning to trust some other spiritual source than ourselves and to lean not on our own understanding and cognition, as it were. But these practices of trust lead us now to the time when we, in humility, can stand before others and begin again, receiving entrance in the community through forgiveness. This is the moment when hiding stages its last stand, coaxing us back into the shadows if we will only feign some generalized sense of sin, but it is now when we are promised that Christ will provide us the healing we seek if only we ask for what we need. And in the asking, we are joined together with the community of Christ.

Confession, like the rest of the practices here, is not "a divine law":[11] it is possible that a person would know the pardon of Christ available to us, without it coming from the outside, having read it in the Scriptures and claimed it for herself. But confession fits a world of speech, a world brought into being by the very Word proceeding from the Father. In the same way that other practices are not laws but gifts, let us beg the question: If it is such a great gift, why would we do without it? It is a peculiar approach that we ask how *little* we must do to be Christians, when the gifts of Christ are so numerous: Why would we not take as many as God offers? Our question then is not *if* confession but *how* confession?

Christ in Community: The Presence of the Lord

Confession, too—though it infuses the other practices of the church-community—is a preparatory practice. The practices of confession

11. Bonhoeffer, *Life Together*, 116.

and communion, in Matthew's Gospel, are tied explicitly together in this way: one cannot enjoy the table of Christ's presence without also being united to the presence of one's sister and brother of the gathered body. It is not by chance that when the former practice is malformed, thought of as amplifications of the individual, the latter is treated as an individually calibrated practice: How could it be anything else?

But the table and the cup have historically for Christians been the center of our gathering together, in that the body of the church gathers around its head, together. The isolating force of sin, present in structure, practice, and habit—and indeed, ritualized both in church and world—is countered in no place more specifically than in this: we cannot enjoy Christ's presence unless we enjoy it together, and we enjoy it reconciled to one another. You may have your arguments and disagreements or you may have Christ; you may have your isolation or you may have Christ; you may not have both.

The vision here is one in which the sacramental character of the gathered body and the presence of Christ in bread and cup are interwoven, as two of the inseparable uses of the name "body of Christ."[12] There is no skipping over the day together, the day apart, or the life of ministry (all places in which our life together is worked out in fear and trembling) in order that one may enjoy the presence of Christ, for the presence of Christ appears not as an invisible, ethereal vapor but under the sign of the bread and the wine—creaturely gifts for creatures on pilgrimage. As we confess to one another, we are offering ourselves in a way befitting the nature of bread and wine—the present and real reconciliation of ourselves to one another and to God, matching the reconciliation that is Christ's own presence.

As Jennifer McBride has characterized it, this is not simply a liturgical act, but one of witness. The church's vocation is one of penitence, but not in a false humility; it is a genuine and grounded work of God's Spirit, with confession as that moment that both gathers in our preparatory work and sends it back out to infuse and deepen

12. For the triplicate modality of this term and how notions of "the real body of Christ" and the "mystical body of Christ" came to be reversed, see Henri de Lubac, *Corpus Mysticum: The Eucharist and the Church in the Middle Ages* (Notre Dame, IN: University of Notre Dame Press, 2016).

our discipleship.[13] Rather, confession should be, McBride argues, the shape of the Christian's public presence because this is the shape of Christ's own reconciling presence. Such a shape is not "apologetic" in the sense of being demure or shy, but it is freely engaging in penitence because it has been forgiven freely by Christ and wishes to "take up space in the world" in this way: expanding the penitence of the world before the Christ who has atoned for it.

Conclusion: The Confessing Church Is the True Church

In confession and Communion, the heart of our life together is made visible, allowing the sin that permeates our life together to gain specific shape in the healing light of the good news. If sin isolates us by keeping our confession generic or invisible, it is in offering our penitent words to another person that we break through to community in Christ with other flesh-and-blood beings. In confession, our sin is made visible, as we know it, so that we might embrace the gospel as we can receive it: "You have been forgiven. Go and sin no more" (cf. John 8:11). Confession and Communion reinfuse our song, our reading, our eating, and our praying by giving a new basis for a shared history together, but one that is simultaneously a work of mission, inviting others into this shared life by its penitence. Thus the church is freed from the burden of being a crowd, from being a performance of perfection, and is enabled to proclaim to the world, "You are a sinner whom Christ forgives. Come be healed and live again."

13. Jennifer McBride, *The Church for the World: A Theology of Public Witness* (Oxford: Oxford University Press, 2012), 179–205, offers a powerful public account of the church offering public repentance for its role in neighborhood decline and having a role to play in neighborhood renewal.

CONCLUSION

AFTER ISOLATION, IN ISOLATION

Living in Christian community is not the kind of inviolable reality that, once put into place, cannot be broken by our practice. Trust can be built and betrayed. Pride can recede and then reenter at a different point. The careful practices of Christian community on their own are fragile, breakable goods, for no structure or practice devoid of the virtues can ever survive long. Christian community, if it is to survive and if it is to offer a future different from the isolation of the past, must constantly be centered in the presence of Christ, putting on the virtues of Christ, receiving the pardon and words of Christ.

It is not a manufacturing plant, in which we put raw people into one end and wait for them to come out of the other end fully mature disciples. It is more akin to growing tomatoes: planting the seeds, watering daily, watching for changes in temperature, paying attention. For in paying attention, we learn to love the particulars and peculiarities of this plant, this patch of ground in which it must take root. Likewise, in the community of Christ, it is a matter of slow attention: as we hear confessions, as we eat together, as we pray, as we sing. We learn from one another, for these people have been given by God and are not a community of our own creation.

The community of Christ, far from gathering in safety, always gathers amid its enemies, for it is there that the Lord anoints with oil and prepares great banquets (cf. Ps. 23:5).[1] And it is in the end that we see that the enemies—whether physical ones or the small and myriad cultural temptations to retreat back into isolation—will not go away. We are to love our enemies and pray for them not only so that they too might join us at the table but also because new enemies continually emerge. We may put off pride, but sloth—not gathering because we lack the courage to hear the voice of our community—will take its place. We may put into practice new ways of praying together or reading Scripture, but the natural strengths of some personalities will always be prone to dominate the meek. The Christian community will always gather amid many other opportunities to retreat back into the crowds.

Doing differently—and indeed, being different—will require us to examine what practices and ministries our churches perform, to look at what technologies have been adopted and what assumptions about being a self have been imbibed, to ask the question of what these have cost us. In what ways are we relying on easy individual consumption of a Christian message to replace the difficulties of Christian community? In what ways are our educational settings and instructional times organized around the free exchange of disposable—and thus trivial—opinions? In what ways do we rely on a common vision, mission, or personality to sustain our church life? In what ways do we assume that if I cannot do precisely what I want by my conscience, I cease to be me?

The enemies to this vision, in the sense of practices gone wild, are legion, but enemies, we are told, are to be loved. They are not to be destroyed so much as rehabilitated, tarried with, rebuked so that they might be gifts instead of dangerous habits to be avoided. And so it is not a matter of, for example, abandoning the media of mass communication so much as recognizing that the media are not value neutral and are not just channels for communicating but that they are shaping *what* the gospel becomes; and it is a matter of determining

1. Dietrich Bonhoeffer, *Life Together*, trans. Daniel W. Bloesch, in *Life Together; Prayerbook of the Bible*, Dietrich Bonhoeffer Works 5 (Minneapolis: Fortress, 1996), 27.

if they can be redeemed. It is a matter not of doing away with people reading the Scriptures alone but rather of helping frame what these times reading Scripture alone *are for.* It is a matter not of having a common vision or mission so much as of remembering that visions die and missions change and pastors retire, yet the church goes on.

In creation, we remain creatures beset by new opportunities to become isolated, and to hide, for we remain sinners called by Christ to be saints. The sin that joins together all humanity, we confess, is matched and overcome by the work Christ has done for all of creation. And so the enemies persist, the challenges remain, and we do not abandon hope. For the Christ whom we know in and through the body—these frail, corporate jars of clay—is the one who has died, has been raised up, and has overcome the world.

The Faith of Christian Community

Christian community is a life that we are joined to not by our own making but by the work of God. Therefore, the faith of the Christian community—which has been entrusted by the church, heard, prayed, and practiced—invites the community to refuse the insularity of autonomy. For it to be a community of Christ is to be joined to all of what Christ is doing, whether or not that specific community recognizes and authorizes it: we are a people on the way, and that way has those before, behind, and beside us.

Isolation, as that which appears under the sign of the individual and of the crowd, appears here to the gathered under the temptation of the *desiccated* body, a body that exists independent and isolated from other Christian bodies. But the Spirit is one who invites our common confession, our common discipleship, and our common prayers, and so the Spirit's invitation is for the community to be permanently opened. This opening is what is necessary for any body to live, for bodies that are sealed off from the outside remain sealed off both from empty, vacuous teaching and from nourishment, both from being contaminated and from ridding contaminants.

The faith of the Christian community is cultivated and nourished in our practices, but it is sustained by what comes from outside, both in our engagements with the creation we share with the world and in the faith that is not parochial to our particular gathering. To be a Christian is to be a catholic Christian, sharing what is common to us as creatures and receiving from beyond our own gathering the gifts that have nourished other Christian communions for generations. The call of Christ into community is not an invitation to disavow what is common and shared but an invitation to hear it and confess it with *this* body, in *this* soil, and in *this* time—not that we might judge it and find it wanting but that we might see the kingdom of God flourish *here* and *now*.

The Love of Christian Community

If the faith that the Christian community confesses is that which is shared—both among its members and with other bodies—then the love it possesses is that by which is it is joined, oriented, and drawn forward in its discipleship. The common danger that comes with Christian community, once begun, is that it will fall back not into the way of the individual but into the way of the crowd. We frequently talk about the way of bearing one another's burdens, of patience, of common prayer, of common confession, but absent a vision of the church being called forward over time, these can become motionless, freezing in amber the love we share to the conditions that made it possible to love—the time, the place, the aesthetics, the people.

As a community grows, it will change, and with that change will come the temptation to limit our love to that which is known already. The love of God is that which stills our wanderings, yet it does so not by letting us remain still but by rightly ordering our journey. The love of God, which leads the church, is for the church's—and the world's—purification. And so the love we share with one another will not allow us simply to enjoy rest that is divorced from that common journey to God. There are thus two parts of the loving call of God: "Your sins are forgiven," and "Go and sin no more." The former statement must come first: the invitation into the life that is given eternally for us and that our life together invites us into, a life out of isolation and into communion with God. But the second is the summons of that life, the call of love to be transformed and to leave behind the isolation in which we will cover ourselves up until we suffocate under the weight of our camouflage. Our love for each other is true when it is this love of Christ, which first sustains us and then draws us further in and on.

The Hope of Christian Community

Isolation goes deep in the human condition, but it is not the first or final word, no matter how it might flourish structurally or shape our imaginations, for God sustains creation and remains present to creation in sin. In light of this, the final word of this meditation on Christian community is simply *patience*. It is no virtue to be patient with those things that are killing us, with sin and vice, but conceptually, we tend to bundle together that which we take as sin with that which we simply have difficulty being close to. What is needed is a vision of church-community as that which Christ is building across time, so that the creation might be redeemed in a way appropriate to the depths to which sin has corrupted our desire for communion. We must be patient, both with others and with ourselves, for Christ remains infinitely patient with us, so that all might come to repentance.[2]

The hope here, as we have noted, is not that in Christian community we will be freed from the enemies who thrive off of division and who make fortunes off of human isolation, for Christ invites us here to love our enemies. The hope here is not that the Christian community will be done with the work of mending, for it is a broken body, one Christ is knitting together of Jews and gentiles, one that will, for all practical purposes, never be finished with its negotiation so long as time exists. And the hope is not that isolation will never again raise its head in Christian community: if anything, I have tried to show that Christian community is never free of isolation as a temptation.

But most chiefly, the hope of Christian community does not rest on it surviving in one form indefinitely. Christian communities, thick

---

2. James Calvin Davis's *Forbearance: A Theological Ethic for a Disagreeable Church* (Grand Rapids: Eerdmans, 2018) rehabilitates patience into forbearance in this ecclesial way, emphasizing the habits and practices that help Christians not only to hear dissent constructively but also to mirror the forbearance that God shows toward sinners.

and robust, faithful and persistent, have been destroyed and swept away by disrepair, decay, or hostility. Longevity is out of our hands, and in any event one does not join something because one knows how long it will endure. The hope of Christian community is that, in this body and as this people, we are participating in the very work of the Spirit in the world: the work of renewing creation, bearing fruit, being witnesses. This hope will one day become sight, as the practices we share and the words we exchange prepare us and shape us for the life to come, one in which Christ will be all in all.

INDEX

Abel, 1
Adam, 1, 26
    character in Genesis, 29–30
    Christ and Adam, 46, 77, 81, 91–92, 166
    "in Adam," 37, 43, 46, 53, 55, 77, 91n6
    inheritance of, 6, 43, 46, 154, 157
    law of, 5, 6
    sin of, 30, 45–46
Anselm of Canterbury, 106
Augustine, 1, 4, 90–91, 98, 133, 161
    City of God, 1, 5, 21–22
    Rule of Saint Augustine, 94
authority
    church, 99, 168–71, 173–74
    interpretive, 58–60

Baptist, 109, 110n37, 112n42
Barringer, Laura, 61, 170–71
Barth, Karl, 40, 52n5, 144
body
    broken, 176, 182
    Holy Spirit, relation to, 42, 80
    human, 26, 35, 114, 116, 118, 128, 136–37, 141
    individuals, relation to, 44–45, 70–71, 74, 95
    mission, 124
    sacrament, 70n1, 74, 110–11, 131, 182, 182n12
    scattered, 59, 70, 99, 128, 138
    social entity, 67, 93, 102, 107, 109, 134, 136, 159, 166, 177
    unity, 51, 61–62, 75, 99, 111n40, 134

    virtual, 33
    See also body of Christ; embodiment
body of Christ
    authority, 169–70
    exemplification of humanity, 10, 14, 19, 99
    gathered, 31–32, 42, 49, 71–74, 82–83, 92, 103, 111, 121, 123–25, 131, 174
    theological concept (church), 10, 37, 47, 92, 94, 106, 108–9, 118, 123, 130, 132, 144, 163, 168, 176
    See also church

Catholicism, Roman, 58n18, 65, 174
    theology, 65, 100, 114
catholicity, 53n7, 99, 133, 188
church
    church-community, 12, 36–37, 47, 53–54, 61, 64, 70, 75, 101, 117, 125–30, 136, 142–43, 148–50, 153, 161–62, 173, 181, 189
    and crowd, 50–55, 60–66, 79, 98, 113, 177–78, 180
    practices. *See* practices: church
    scattered, 13–14, 54, 59, 95, 99, 122–23, 125, 128, 136, 138
communion
    bodily, 32, 71–72, 114
    church, 84
    union with God, 2, 12–14, 22n13, 45, 59, 188
    union with others, x, 3, 6, 13–14, 19–20, 26–27, 69, 83, 86, 115, 154, 159, 162–63, 188–89